THE LOOP HOLE

Unveiling the story behind Jesus' teachings on adulterous marriages, divorce & remarriage

DARIUS GOOD

DEDICATION

To the woman from Adelaide, South Australia – though our encounter was brief, it profoundly reshaped my perspective and the understanding of the impact of my research and the ministry.

Be blessed.

TABLE OF CONTENTS

IT NEVER MADE SENSE

In 2021, an unexpected hospital visit led to surgery, and I found myself on bed rest for six weeks. I stepped away from my pastoral duties to give my body the time it needed to heal. Never one to sit idle, a question kept stirring in my mind: What did divorce look like during Jesus' time? More specifically, I was curious about the legal process. Did people go to court? Did they appear before a judge? What exactly did a bill of divorce look like?

I couldn't find answers to these questions in Scripture. At the time, I assumed the Bible said very little about divorce—but I was deeply mistaken. I had heard ministers teach that men could divorce their wives simply by saying, "I divorce you," three times. Later, I learned this wasn't true. That wasn't a practice used in Israel. It didn't take long into my studies to realize that much of what I had been taught on the subject was inaccurate.

As a pastor's son, church was part of our weekly routine. Though my father never preached about divorce, I grew up surrounded by the popular teachings on the topic. Yet, none of them seemed to make sense. I struggled to reconcile how Jesus could say divorce was only permissible in the case of adultery—especially when adultery was punishable by death under Israelite law. I kept asking: Why was adultery the only "just" cause for divorce? Why wasn't abuse or abandonment included? Even in my youth, these teachings felt incomplete and unjust. Still, the common Christian response I received was, "We don't talk about divorce. It's not an option, so there's no need to discuss it."

But as I lay in bed recovering from surgery, that question wouldn't leave me alone. So, I began to dig deeper. I read Christian perspectives on divorce, but they echoed what I had always heard: that remarriage after divorce was essentially adultery. My search eventually led me to several Hebrew terms, which then directed me to a Jewish encyclopedia. That's when everything began to shift. I discovered that every Jewish couple was required by law to have a ketubah—a formal prenuptial agreement. This document outlined the husband's obligations and even detailed how a divorce should be handled.

The more I studied, the more I realized how flawed and often uninformed many Christian teachings on divorce truly are—especially when it comes to interpreting the law of Moses. As I began to grasp the law in its proper context, Jesus' words started to make much more sense. However, I also noticed a troubling pattern: there appeared to be a "Christianized version" of the Mosaic law that stood in contrast to what Jewish tradition and interpretation actually taught.

To properly understand Jesus' statements, we must first understand the law He was referring to. The real issue lies in the widespread lack of knowledge about the law of Moses. As the Apostle Paul put it:

1 Timothy 1:7 (AMP):
"[They are] wanting to be teachers of the Law [of Moses], even though they do not understand the terms they use or the subjects about which they make [such] confident declarations."

About three years into my studies, I finally found an answer to another question that had bothered me: Why did Jesus focus so much on adulterous marriages? I wondered if this was a major issue in Israel at the time. Eventually, I discovered the reason—and it brought everything into sharp focus. Jewish men had found a way to legally sidestep the Mosaic laws surrounding divorce. What they were doing wasn't illegal, but it was deeply unethical. The problem had become so widespread that the Jewish

Supreme Court—the Sanhedrin—had to step in and pass additional laws to close this loophole.

Jesus' teachings on divorce and remarriage suddenly became crystal clear: He was addressing the very abuse and exploitation of the law that men were using to their advantage. These were laws that Israelite women were not legally permitted to exercise.

Before diving into the divorce trends in ancient Israel and how they circumvented the law of Moses, we need to understand some foundational concepts: key Hebrew terms, cultural practices, and legal definitions. Many words we use today—like "adultery," "adulterous marriage," or "divorce"—don't carry the same meaning they did in ancient Israel. We cannot simply look up words in Hebrew or Greek, apply their definitions, and expect to gain a proper understanding of an ancient society. Too often, the Old Testament is taught through the lens of modern or Western perspectives, rather than from the viewpoint of those who actually lived during that time.

Marriage, divorce, and adultery in biblical Israel are complex subjects—so much so that they could easily form the curriculum of a 12-week university course. In fact, this would fall under the category of "Family Law in Ancient Israel." To study family law in America requires nearly seven years of education, including law school. That tells you how intricate and layered the topic is.

I'll do my best to condense years of research into something more accessible. I've included Hebrew terms and their definitions as understood by both the Mosaic law and the Jewish court system (the Sanhedrin). Gaining clarity on these terms will shed tremendous light on Jesus' teachings about divorce, adultery, and remarriage—and even reshape how we interpret certain Bible stories we thought we understood.

We'll also take a look at how Israelite men manipulated legal loopholes and how the Sanhedrin responded to this trend. In doing so, we'll come to see that Jesus' teachings didn't contradict the law of Moses at all—they upheld it, challenged its abuse, and called the people back to its heart.

SOUND DOCTRINE

It is commonly taught that Jesus restricted the law of Moses, permitting divorce only in cases of adultery. This teaching implies that Jesus altered the Mosaic law—the original law contained no such limitation. As a result, many have come to believe that Jesus "clarified" the law or revealed God's true intention behind it.

In some Christian circles, it's popularly believed that Jesus came to "fix" the law of Moses and introduce a new doctrine centered on love, grace, and mercy—as if the Mosaic law lacked these qualities. This perspective has led many to see a sharp contrast between the teachings of Jesus and the law of Moses, often overlooking Jesus' own words where He clearly stated that He did not come to destroy the law. Some even misinterpret Matthew 5:17 to mean something entirely different from what Jesus actually said.

Matthew 5:17 (KJV)
"Think not that I am come to destroy the law, or the prophets:
I am not come to destroy, but to fulfil."

Jesus' teachings were not in contradiction to the law of Moses. On the contrary, He emphasized that He did not come to change or abolish it. In fact, Jesus made several key statements that affirm the significance and divine origin of the law.

"He [Moses] wrote of Me."

Jesus revealed that the law of Moses was ultimately written about Him and pointed to His coming.

John 5:46 (KJV)
"For had ye believed Moses, ye would have believed me: for *he wrote of me*."

Luke 24:44 (KJV)
"And he said unto them, These are the words which I spake unto you, while I was yet with you, that all things must be fulfilled, which were *written in the law of Moses*, and in the prophets, and in the psalms, *concerning me*."

If the law was written about Jesus and pointed to His mission, why would He need to change it? The most common explanation I've heard is that Moses added certain things to the law which Jesus later corrected. But if that were true, it would mean that Moses defiled God's Word with his additions—a serious accusation. While Moses physically wrote the law, he was not its author. The law was given to Moses by God Himself.

In Ephesians 4:14, Paul admonishes the church in Ephesius not to remain immature in the faith—like ships, tossed back and forth by every "wind of doctrine". Many teachings in the church today are built from fragments of truth, much like puzzle pieces that may fit part of the picture but fail to connect with the whole. Before we examine Jewish culture and laws, we must first establish truth that is grounded in sound doctrine.

The Law is One Law

The law of Moses consists of laws, statutes, ordinances, and precepts—but it is treated as one unified law. That's why it's referred to as "the law of Moses" rather than "the laws of Moses." Breaking even a single part of it was regarded as breaking the entire law (see Deuteronomy 17:19; 27:26; 28:58; 31:12; and James 2:10). The covenant made between Israel and God required full obedience to the entire law—not selective adherence. This is the same truth that James later reaffirmed:

James 2:10 (Complete Jewish Bible)
"For a person who keeps the whole Torah, yet stumbles at one
point, has become guilty of breaking them all."

Moses Was the Mediator, Not the Author of the Law

Some argue—and entire books have been written to support this claim—that there's a distinction between the Law of the Lord (often identified as the Ten Commandments) and the Law of Moses (viewed as separate and flawed). This viewpoint holds that Moses added his own laws and that Jesus came to correct those additions. However, this doctrine is flawed.

Scripture clarifies that Moses was the mediator—not the creator—of the law. The law was given by God and delivered to Moses through the agency of angels.

Galatians 3:19 (NLT)
"Why, then, was the law given? It was given alongside the promise
to show people their sins. But the law was designed to last only
until the coming of the child who was promised. ***God gave his
law through angels to Moses***, who was the mediator between
God and the people."

When God called Moses up Mount Sinai, He made it clear that He would give him not only the tables of stone—which included the Ten Commandments—but also a law and commandments that God Himself had written. This is significant for anyone trying to separate the "law" from the "commandments."

Exodus 24:12 (KJV)
"And the Lord said unto Moses, Come up to me into the mount,
and be there: and I will give thee tables of stone, and a law, and
commandments which I have written; that thou mayest teach
them."

Both the law and the commandments came directly from God. Moses did not create them—he was the one chosen to receive and teach them.

The Law is Perfect

If Jesus came to "fix" the law of Moses, it would suggest that the law was flawed. But the law of Moses was not flawed—it was perfect because it came directly from God, just as the commandments did.

Psalm 19:7 (KJV)
The law of the Lord is perfect, converting the soul: the testimony
of the Lord is sure, making wise the simple.

The law is holy

The law is holy. If Moses had changed or added anything to it, the law would no longer be holy—it would have been defiled and tainted by man. Paul affirms the holiness of the law in Romans 7:12, where he also declares that the commandment is holy, just, and good:

Romans 7:12
"Wherefore the law is holy, and the commandment holy, and just, and good."

In Hebrews 8:5, Paul explains that God admonished Moses to construct the Tabernacle exactly according to the pattern shown to him on Mount Sinai. Moses was given precise instructions and was not allowed to alter or add to the design. In the same way, Moses was not permitted to add any laws to those given by God.

Many of the commandments from the Law of Moses, instituted by Moses, were actually traditions, practices, and cultural norms, such as tithing and Levirate marriage, that were practiced by the fathers— Abraham, Isaac, Jacob, and the other patriarchs and matriarchs. Jesus highlights this truth during one of His debates with the Pharisees. He points out that the law of circumcision, though attributed to Moses, originated with the fathers.

John 7:22 (KJV)
Moses therefore gave unto you circumcision; (*not because it is of Moses, but of the fathers*;) and ye on the sabbath day circumcise a man.

Are the Law and the Commandments Not the Same?

Some argue that there is a clear distinction between the law of God and the law of Moses, often based on selective interpretations of scripture. For instance, some point to Psalm 19:7, claiming that it praises only the law of the Lord—not the law of Moses. However, they often overlook the very next verse, which speaks of the statutes of the Lord:

Psalm 19:7-8
7. *The law of the Lord is perfect*, converting the soul: the testimony of the Lord is sure, making wise the simple.
8. *The statutes of the LORD are right*, rejoicing the heart: the commandment of the LORD is pure, enlightening the eyes.

Those who promote this distinction frequently cannot define what the "statutes of the Lord" are—yet these very statutes are laid out in the law of Moses.

The law of Moses included 613 commandments, made up of laws, statutes, ordinances, and precepts. For example:

- A statute: The law against breeding different kinds of livestock (Leviticus 19:19)
- Another statute: The command prohibiting priests from drinking wine or strong drink (Leviticus 10:9)
- An ordinance: The command to observe the Feast of Unleavened Bread (Exodus 12:17)

- A precept: The legal process for divorce, including the requirement for a bill of divorcement (Deuteronomy 24:1-4)

Jesus Himself referred to this precept in Mark 10:4–5:

> 4. And they said, Moses suffered to write a bill of divorcement, and to put [her] away.
> 5. And Jesus answered and said unto them, For the hardness of your heart he wrote you ***this precept***.

Although some claim that Moses wrote the precept and not God, the truth is that Moses only wrote what God instructed him to write. All laws, statutes, ordinances, and precepts originated from God.

> Nehemiah 9:14
> "And madest known unto them thy holy sabbath, and
> ***commandedst them precepts, statutes, and laws***, by the hand
> of Moses thy servant."

The Ten Commandments Spoken to Israel at Mount Sinai

When people think of Moses receiving the Ten Commandments, they often picture him climbing Mount Sinai and receiving two stone tablets from God. This is partly drawn from Exodus 24:12 (KJV):

> "And the LORD said unto Moses, Come up to me into the mount, and be there: and I will give thee tables of stone, and a law, and commandments which I have written; that thou mayest teach them."

However, a detail many misunderstand is that the Ten Commandments were first given verbally in Exodus 20, before God inscribed them on stone tablets.

In Exodus 19, God instructed Moses to gather the elders and the people and sanctify them. God announced that He would come down in a thick cloud so the people could hear His voice, confirming that Moses was indeed speaking on God's authority. A boundary was set around Mount Sinai, and anyone who touched the mountain was to be put to death.

When God descended in Exodus 19:16, there was lightning, thunder, and a thick cloud that covered the mountain, with fire and smoke ascending like a great furnace. Then God began to speak, delivering the Ten Commandments to the entire nation (Exodus 20:1–17). The people were terrified and backed away from the mountain.

Afterward, Moses alone approached the thick darkness covering the mountain as the people watched. God then began to speak directly to him, giving the ordinances beginning in Exodus 20:22.

Exodus 21:1 (AMP) "Now these are the ordinances (laws) which you shall set before the Israelites:"

These ordinances included instructions on building altars, repayment of debts through servitude, handling personal injuries (including manslaughter and murder), consequences for causing premature birth, property rights, theft, and more. God also established three national feasts:

1. Feast of Unleavened Bread (Passover)
2. Feast of Harvest (Weeks/Pentecost/Firstfruits)
3. Feast of Ingathering (Tabernacles/Booths/Sukkot)

The Lord concluded speaking in Exodus 23:33. It was after this that God called Moses, along with Aaron, Nadab, Abihu, and seventy elders, to ascend the mountain. Moses then rehearsed God's words to the people, and they agreed to the covenant (Exodus 24:7). Only in verses 12–13 does Moses ascend to the mountain to receive the stone tablets.

These details are important because they clarify a common misconception: God gave Moses the Ten Commandments, but all the other ordinances, statutes, and precepts were created by Moses. This teaching contradicts the scriptures; God spoke many of the ordinances to

Moses in front of the nation of Israel. The dramatic display of fire, lightning, dark clouds, and smoke revealed to the nation of Israel that Moses was indeed speaking with God. Moses was not inventing laws to govern Israel—he was faithfully conveying God's instructions to the people.

God Corrected Moses, Aaron, and Miriam

God didn't hesitate to correct those closest to Him when they disobeyed. He struck Miriam with leprosy for her attitude toward Moses' wife. He killed Aaron's sons, Nadab and Abihu, for failing to follow priestly commandments—and He even told Aaron he was not allowed to mourn them. When Moses struck the rock instead of speaking to it, his disobedience cost him entrance into the Promised Land.

If God held them accountable in these ways, why would He overlook supposed flaws in the law for over a thousand years—until Jesus arrived to "fix" it?

Jesus did Not do Away with Capital Punishment

In classical Jewish law (Halacha), the Talmud identifies 36 capital offenses—crimes punishable by death—derived from the Torah (Pentateuch). These offenses are explicitly listed in rabbinic sources such as Mishnah Sanhedrin 7:4 and are further detailed in the Talmud (Sanhedrin 49a–83b). The capital crimes include acts such as idolatry, sexual immorality (including adultery, incest, and bestiality), Sabbath desecration, blasphemy, murder, kidnapping, false prophecy, and other severe transgressions against God and society.

Some Christian teachings claim that Jesus abolished capital punishment, suggesting that He reduced adultery from a capital offense to a moral offense that allows for divorce rather than execution. This argument, however, is inconsistent when applied to other capital crimes such as murder, rape, and kidnapping, which remain universally recognized as severe offenses. Proponents of this view often also believe that the Sanhedrin was a "bloody court" eager to execute offenders. In reality, the Sanhedrin rarely carried out the death penalty. The Talmud (Makkot 7a) teaches that a Sanhedrin that executed even once in seven years (or seventy years, according to another opinion) was considered "bloody," underscoring the extreme caution Jewish courts exercised in capital cases.

Jesus did not diminish adultery or make it a lesser crime. However, the confusion lies in the understanding that an adulterous marriage is not the same as an individual committing the physical act of adultery, according to the Law of Moses. In His teachings on divorce, Jesus was not providing a list of "just causes" for divorce. This is why He did not mention other legitimate grounds, such as physical or emotional abuse, which were already addressed and condemned under the Law of Moses. The Mishnah (Ketubot 7:9) and Talmud (Ketubot 72a-77a) discuss scenarios where a Beit Din (rabbinical court) could compel a man to divorce his wife if he mistreated her. We see Laban telling Jacob not to abuse his daughters in Genesis 31:50. Instead, Jesus was specifically addressing the issue of adulterous marriages—a distinct legal category separate from the act of adultery. The penalty for entering an adulterous marriage was not capital punishment but carried serious civil consequences, particularly regarding financial settlements, inheritance rights, and marital status. Jesus was addressing this issue because adulterous marriages were widespread across Israel due to Jewish men exploiting legal loopholes to bypass God's law.

Paul Used the Law to Reveal Christ

Some people use Paul's teachings to argue that Jesus contradicted the law. But in Acts 28:23, we see Paul using both the law and the prophets to point people to Jesus:

Acts 28:23 (KJV)
"And when they had appointed him a day, there came many to him

into his lodging; to whom he expounded and testified the
kingdom of God, persuading them concerning Jesus, both ***out of
the law of Moses***, and out of the prophets, from morning till
evening."

Paul didn't set the law aside—he used it to reveal Christ. The law doesn't oppose Jesus; it points to Him.

Shadows Must Reflect the Image

Hebrews 8:5 explains that the law (the old covenant) was a shadow or example of things to come (the new covenant). A shadow must resemble the very thing it reflects. Yet, many Christian teachings about Christ bear little to no resemblance to the law of Moses. The Old Testament serves as the example—the pattern—that the New Testament follows. However, modern Christian doctrine often presents the two covenants as opposing or contradictory.

Jesus told Nicodemus that to understand spiritual things, one must first grasp the natural:

John 3:12 (NIV)
"I have spoken to you of earthly things and you do not believe;
how then will you believe if I speak of heavenly things?"

There must be harmony between the natural example and the spiritual reality. The law of Moses represents the natural experiences—the "earthly things"—while the kingdom of God reflects the "heavenly things." The two are meant to align, not conflict.

Jesus Taught the Law of Moses

A very common teaching in the Christian community is that the Pharisees taught the law of Moses, adhering to the legality of the law, whereas Jesus taught a deeper understanding of the law. This conclusion is inaccurate, and the scriptures explain that Jesus taught the law, whereas the Pharisees taught tradition.

John 7:19 (KJV)
Did not Moses give you the law, and [yet] none of you keepeth the law? Why go ye about to kill me?

The Pharisees told Jesus that His disciples broke the traditions of their fathers by eating with unwashed hands. There is no law in the law of Moses stating hands must be washed before eating, which Jesus explained to them in Mark 7:1-5.

Another major tradition Jesus corrected was the "Corban" rule—a man-made tradition that allowed people to neglect caring for their parents by claiming their money or possessions were "dedicated to God." The concept of dedicating offerings (Corban, Korban, or Qorban) to God was valid, but the abuse of this practice allowed some to sidestep their obligations to their parents under the guise of religious devotion. Jesus explained this tradition violated the law honor thy father and mother.

Matthew 15:6 (KJV)
And honour not his father or his mother, [he shall be free]. ***Thus have ye made the commandment of God of none effect by your tradition***.

Jesus rebuked the Pharisees for teaching and elevating tradition above God's law, and not for their strict keeping of the law. It was Jesus who taught the law of Moses and not the Pharisees. You do not find Jesus correcting the Sadducees. The Sadducees did not rely on oral tradition or elaborate religious customs or elevating tradition over Scripture like the Pharisees did. Jesus corrected the Sadducees over their rejected belief in angels, spirits, and the resurrection of the dead (Matthew 22, Acts 23:8). Rather than rebuking their traditions, Jesus rebuked their ignorance of Scripture and their theological errors.

The Greatest Commandment is the Law of Moses

It's commonly taught that Jesus came to introduce new laws, but this is not accurate. When Jesus spoke of the greatest commandments, He was not establishing new ones—He was quoting from the law of Moses:

Matthew 22:37–40 (KJV)

37. Jesus said unto him, Thou shalt love the Lord thy God with all thy heart, and with all thy soul, and with all thy mind.

38. This is the first and great commandment.

39. And the second is like unto it, Thou shalt love thy neighbour as thyself.

40. On these two commandments hang all the law and the prophets.

These commandments were already written in the Old Testament:

- Leviticus 19:18 (KJV): Thou shalt not avenge, nor bear any grudge against the children of thy people, but thou shalt love thy neighbour as thyself: I am the Lord.

- Deuteronomy 6:5 (KJV): And thou shalt love the Lord thy God with all thine heart, and with all thy soul, and with all thy might.

Jesus made it clear that these two commandments were foundational—yet they were not part of the Ten Commandments. They came from the broader law given through Moses.

Even when tempted by Satan, Jesus responded with the words, "It is written," quoting the law of Moses—Deuteronomy 8:3; 6:13; 6:16. His teachings never opposed the law; they confirmed and upheld it.

The Sermon on the Mount largely reframes familiar Old Testament themes. For instance, when Jesus declares in Matthew 5:5, 'Blessed are the meek, for they shall inherit the earth,' he's not quoting Psalm 37:11 verbatim, but his statement affirms this spiritual ideal. Perceived conflicts between Jesus' teachings in the Sermon on the Mount and the Law of

Moses typically arise from a lack of familiarity and understanding of the Mosaic Law.

The Greatest and the Least Laws

Many Christian teachings are riddled with confusion because the structure of the Law of Moses is often misunderstood. The laws were not all equal in weight; they were arranged from least to greatest, and some laws superseded others in authority. Without grasping this principle, it is easy to misinterpret Jesus' interactions with the Pharisees and scribes as though He were bypassing or violating the Mosaic law.

Near the beginning of the Sermon on the Mount, Jesus referred to the "least commandments":

Matthew 5:19 (KJV)
"Whosoever therefore shall break one of these least commandments, and shall teach men so, he shall be called the least in the kingdom of heaven: but whosoever shall do and teach [them], the same shall be called great in the kingdom of heaven."

The Sermon on the Mount focused on these "lesser" commandments— not introducing new ones, but calling for their proper observance. When Jesus said, "But I say to you," He was not replacing God's law, but admonishing His listeners to keep the law in its entirety, including laws often neglected, such as the prohibition against coveting a neighbor's wife (Exodus 20:17, Matthew 5:28).

Matthew 5:21, Jesus began by quoting Moses' commandment, "You shall not kill." He did not void, replace, or add to this law. Rather, He emphasized that verbal mistreatment—such as calling someone "Raca" or "fool" (Matthew 5:22)—was itself a serious offense that could bring a person before a Jewish court. This teaching aligns with the Torah's command against harmful speech (Lashon HaRa) in Leviticus 19:16, which rabbinic tradition expands into five categories of forbidden speech:

1. Lashon HaRa — "Evil Speech" (Leviticus 19:16)
2. Rechilut — "Talebearing" / Gossip (Leviticus 19:16)
3. Motzi Shem Ra — "Spreading a Bad Name" / Slander (Deuteronomy 22:13–19)
4. Ona'at Devarim — "Verbal Oppression" / Hurtful Speech (Leviticus 25:17)
5. Nivul Peh — "Obscene Speech" / Vulgar Talk (Deuteronomy 23:10–15)

Though the Torah did not explicitly prescribe punishment for insults, rabbinic tradition regarded verbal humiliation (ona'at devarim—"verbal mistreatment") as a grave offense. A Beit Din was authorized to address such transgressions, sometimes using strict measures like admonitory lashes, fines, or requiring public apologies. Bava Metzia 58b states: "He who publicly shames his neighbor is as though he shed blood." Embarrassment was seen as socially destructive, threatening both community honor and personal dignity. A person who publicly demeaned another with contemptuous words could be brought before a Jewish court for judgment, because it was considered a moral injury akin to violence. The Talmud reinforces this, stating that verbal mistreatment can be even worse than financial fraud because emotional damage is harder to repair.

The Pharisees accused Jesus' disciples of breaking the Sabbath by plucking corn in Matthew 12:1-2. Jesus defended their innocence by citing examples of laws that superseded the Sabbath. He reminded the Pharisees that David ate the consecrated showbread, which was normally reserved for priests (Matthew 12:3–4; cf. 1 Samuel 21:6). He also reminded them that the priests "profane the Sabbath" in the Temple (Matthew 12:5) by performing their required duties, yet are guiltless.

Though violating the Sabbath was a capital offense (Exodus 31:14–15), certain commandments outranked it. In Jewish law (Halakha), the principle of Pikuach Nefesh—the preservation of human life (Leviticus

18:5)—overrides almost every other commandment, including Sabbath observance, fasting, and most ritual restrictions. The Priest was permitted to give David the consecrated shewbread, not because David was anointed or a priest, as some Christians mistakenly teach, but because of this law. David's men also ate the shewbread, and they held no royal or priestly status, which further confirms that their lives being in danger was the true reason the bread could be lawfully given.

Priests were required to work on the Sabbath by offering double sacrifices (Numbers 28:9–10) and replacing (baking) the showbread (Leviticus 24:8; 1 Chronicles 9:32), but in doing so, they were "blameless" (Matthew 12:5). The same was true for circumcision. The Brit Milah (covenant of circumcision, Leviticus 12:3) was performed on the eighth day, even if it fell on the Sabbath or Yom Kippur. While not a life-saving act, it was considered a "time-specific commandment of covenant (***mitzvot aseh sheha'zman gerama***)" that overrode Sabbath restrictions. (Jewish law has time-specific commandment of covenant and time-bound commandments of covenant (mitzvah be-zeman berit or mitzvot et berit)). Jesus referenced this in John 7:22-24, arguing that if the Law permits circumcision on the Sabbath in observance of the law, then healing a man on the Sabbath—making him "every whit whole"—is even more justified:

John 7:23
If a man on the sabbath day receive circumcision, that the law of Moses should not be broken; are ye angry at me, because I have made a man every whit whole on the sabbath day?

Far from breaking the Law, Jesus operated fully within its structure. He understood which commandments were greater and which were lesser, and upheld them accordingly. This is why, when asked which commandment was the greatest, He quoted Deuteronomy 6:5 and Leviticus 19:18—the commandments to love God and love one's neighbor—because all other laws find their proper place under these two.

Love Your Enemies

Matthew 5:43-44 (KJV)
43. Ye have heard that it hath been said, Thou shalt love thy neighbour, and hate thine enemy.
44. But I say unto you, Love your enemies, bless them that curse you, do good to them that hate you, and pray for them which despitefully use you, and persecute you;

When Jesus commanded us to love our enemies, He was not contradicting or correcting the Law of Moses. The Torah never instructed Israel to hate their enemies — quite the opposite. Several laws required compassion even toward an enemy: helping them when in trouble (Exodus 23:4–5), refusing to seek revenge or hold grudges (Leviticus 19:17–18), and even feeding and giving water to an enemy (Proverbs 25:21–22), which Paul later quoted in Romans 12:20. Jesus' statement addressed a distorted mindset that limited the word "neighbor" to fellow Israelites or converts, which led some to believe it was acceptable to mistreat outsiders. This interpretation was contrary to the Law of Moses, which explicitly said, "Do not despise an Edomite, for he is your brother" (Deuteronomy 23:7). In addition, a sectarian Jewish group known as the Essenes taught, "They shall love all the sons of light... and hate all the sons of darkness" (Community Rule, 1QS 1:9–11). The Qumran community saw themselves as God's chosen remnant and considered everyone else "sons of darkness," which justified hostility toward them. Jesus rejected this interpretation and restored the Torah's heart of mercy and love.

Jesus further corrected this line of thinking when asked by a lawyer in Luke 10:29, "Who is my neighbor?" Jesus tells the parable of a man who was robbed and badly injured. A priest and Levite walked past the fellow Israelite, but a non-Israelite (Samaritan) was more neighborly, taking the man to be cared for.

You Can Not Add to or Cancel a Covenant

To think that the covenant God made with the nation of Israel at Mount Sinai could simply be altered by Jesus — without Israel's consent — is not how covenants or legal agreements work. Jesus could not come and make changes to an already established covenant. Paul actually made this very argument to the churches in Galatia:

Galatians 3:15 (KJV)
Brethren, I speak after the manner of men; Though it be but a man's covenant, yet if it be confirmed, no man disannulleth, or addeth thereto.

Paul is saying, "Let's use an everyday example: even in the case of human covenants, once the agreement has been confirmed, no one can cancel it ('disannulleth') or add to it ('addeth thereto')."

Other translations make this even clearer:

Galatians 3:15 (NLT)
Dear brothers and sisters, here's an example from everyday life. Just as no one can set aside or amend an irrevocable agreement, so it is in this case.

Galatians 3:15 (AMP)
Brothers and sisters, I speak in terms of human relations: even though a last will and testament is just a human covenant, yet when it has been signed and made legally binding, no one sets it aside or adds to it [modifying it in some way].

A covenant can't simply be canceled (annulled) or changed by one party. But it can come to an end (be completed) in one of three main ways, depending on the type of covenant:

1. Fulfillment (Completion of Terms) – Numbers 6:13
2. Death of One Party (Testament Analogy) - Romans 7:1-4
3. Covenant Breach (Breaking It and Suffering Consequences) - Numbers 14:34, Deuteronomy 28, Hosea 6:7 (Adam)

Paul's point is clear: the Law, which came 430 years after God's covenant with Abraham, did not annul or alter that covenant. In the same way, Jesus' coming did not cancel or change the Law of Moses.

Jesus Did Not and Could Not End the Law

God made several perpetual covenants in Scripture — the Abrahamic covenant, the kingship of David's line, and the Mosaic covenant. This means the Law of Moses was described as everlasting (Exodus 31:16–17, Leviticus 16:29–34, Exodus 27:20–21, Leviticus 3:17, Leviticus 24:8, Numbers 18:19, 2 Chronicles 33:8).

Jesus confirmed this when He said the Law would remain until heaven and earth pass away and until it has fulfilled its purpose (Matthew 5:18). The Law's purpose is to reveal sin (Romans 7:7) and define transgressions (Galatians 3:19). The law was given to make people accountable and to lead us to Christ.

A perpetual law can never end, so when Paul writes in Romans 10:4 that "Christ is the end of the law," he does not mean the Law ceased to exist. The word "end" here means goal, aim, or culmination — Christ is the destination toward which the Law was always pointing. John confirms this when he writes that "the Word became flesh and dwelt among us" (John 1:14). Jesus was the living embodiment of the Law (Torah) and the Prophets — the perfect example of what God intends for His people through the help of the Holy Spirit.

1 Peter 2:21-23 (KJV)
21 For even hereunto were ye called: because ***Christ also suffered for us, leaving us an example, that ye should follow his steps***:
22 Who ***did no sin, neither was guile*** found in his mouth:
23 Who, when he was reviled, ***reviled not again***; when he suffered, he ***threatened not***; but ***committed [himself] to him that judgeth righteously***:

Jesus' coming and death did not bring an end to the Mosaic covenant, yet believers are no longer under the law. The question then is: how does this covenant end for us? God did not end it by simply declaring it fulfilled or by allowing us to break it — He ended it by death, our deaths. Scripture teaches that we die to the Law through the death of Christ and are raised with Him. This death frees us from the first covenant and allows us to enter into the new covenant. The Law still remains, but through our death with Christ we are no longer under its authority, requirements, restrictions, or curses.

Romans 7:4 (KJV)
Wherefore, my brethren, *ye also are become dead to the law by the body of Christ*; that ye should be married to another, [even] to him who is raised from the dead, that we should bring forth fruit unto God.

Romans 7:6 (NLT)
But now we have been released from the law, for *we died to it and are no longer captive to its power*. Now we can serve God, not in the old way of obeying the letter of the law, but in the new way of living in the Spirit.

Galatians 2:20 (KJV)
I am crucified with Christ: nevertheless I live; yet not I, but Christ liveth in me: and the life which I now live in the flesh I live by the faith of the Son of God, who loved me, and gave himself for me.

2 Timothy 2:11 (KJV)
It is a faithful saying: For if *we be dead with him*, we shall also live with him.

The Law Was Made Complete (Fulfilled)

When Jesus said He came to "fulfill the law," many interpret this to mean that He brought it to an end. However, "fulfill" can also mean to complete or bring to fullness. Jesus came to complete what the law and prophets had pointed toward.

He is the Passover Lamb (John 1:29, Acts 8:32)—He had to die during the Feast of Unleavened Bread (Luke 22), and His bones could not be broken (John 19:36), in alignment with the law (Exodus 12:46). He was the bread (manna) from heaven (John 6:51) and the rock that provided water (John 4:14). He was the brazen serpent that was lifted up on the pole in the wilderness (John 3:14). His body was the temple (Mark 15:58) and the veil (Exodus 26:33, Hebrews 10:20). He is the high priest (Hebrews 4:14) and the scapegoat (Leviticus 16:8, John 18:38-39). The *mikvah* was required for spiritual cleansing (Leviticus 11:36), but now we are cleansed by His Word (Ephesians 5:26), His blood (Revelation 1:5), and through fellowship (1 John 1:7). He is our Sabbath, our rest (Hebrews 4), and the fulfillment of so much more that was associated with the Law of Moses. In many ways, Jesus became the embodiment of the Law itself. All the religious requirements of the Law are fulfilled in Jesus Christ. If He had contradicted the Law, He could not have fulfilled it. Christ was a sacrificial lamb, unblemished and spotless (1 Peter 1:19).

Paul also explained that the culmination—the true goal—of the law is love from a pure heart:

1 Timothy 1:5
Now the end of the commandment is charity out of a pure heart,
and of a good conscience, and of faith unfeigned.

This was the entire purpose behind the 613 commandments: to teach people how to love one another. Paul echoed this in Galatians 5:22–23, when he wrote that there is no law against the fruit of the Spirit—love, joy, peace, patience, and so on. These are the very qualities the law was meant to produce.

A World Without Laws

If we truly loved one another—without grudges or vengeance, as Leviticus 19:18 instructs—the law would become unnecessary. The courts would be empty. Judges and lawyers would have no cases to try. The entire legal system would be without purpose.

But that's not the world we live in. People still lack love, compassion, and humility. That's why the law remains necessary. As Paul states:

1 Timothy 1:9
The law was not made for a righteous man, but for the lawless and disobedient...

The law served as God's standard for justice. If people had acted with a pure conscience—doing what was right in God's eyes instead of their own—the law would not have been needed.

Jesus is the Living Expression of the Law

Jesus was the embodiment of the love God desires us to show one another. He is what the law looks like when it is truly kept. When we live by the Spirit of Christ—the Holy Spirit—we walk in love, truth, and righteousness. And when we are led by the Spirit, we are no longer under the law, not because the law is abolished, but because we fulfill it through love.

Galatians 5:18
But if ye be led of the Spirit, ye are not under the law.

Romans 13:8
Owe no man any thing, but to love one another: for he that loveth another hath fulfilled the law.

Romans 13:10
Love worketh no ill to his neighbour: therefore love is the fulfilling of the law.

The Law Was Given for Order—Not Justification

God gave the law to the nation of Israel to establish a system of justice and order. Every citizen—whether native-born or foreign—was expected to abide by it, Exodus 12:49. Like any functioning nation, Israel needed a government and a legal structure. At Mount Sinai, God established both. But the law was never meant to make people righteous.

Paul made this clear when he wrote that if righteousness could have come through a law, then God would have given one that could impart life:

Galatians 3:21 (KJV)
Is the law then against the promises of God? God forbid: for if there had been a law given which could have given life, verily righteousness should have been by the law.

Galatians 3:21 (NLT)
Is there a conflict, then, between God's law and God's promises? Absolutely not! If the law could give us new life, we could be made right with God by obeying it.

Jesus Fulfilled the Law Through Faith, Not Works

Jesus fulfilled the law by adding the one critical element it lacked: faith as the path to righteousness. The law was never designed to make people righteous. It governed behavior, established justice, and maintained order within the nation of Israel—but it could not justify anyone before God. True righteousness comes only through faith in Jesus Christ. His death satisfied the requirements of the law—such as atonement and ransom—and brought justification to all who believe.

Galatians 2:16 (KJV)
Knowing that *a man is not justified by the works of the law, but by the faith of Jesus Christ*, even we have believed in Jesus Christ, that we might be justified by the faith of Christ, and not by the works of the law: for by the works of the law shall no flesh be justified.

Galatians 3:11 (KJV)
But that ***no man is justified by the law*** in the sight of God, it is
evident: for, ***The just shall live by faith***.

We must take Jesus at His word when He said He made no changes to
the law of Moses.

Matthew 5:17 (KJV)
"Think not that I am come to destroy the law, or the prophets: I
am not come to destroy, but to fulfil."

Seeing the Law Through a Jewish Lens

To better understand how Jesus and the law of Moses align, we need to
see the law through the eyes of its original audience: the Jewish people.
Their culture, customs, and interpretation of the law provide context that
is often lost in modern explanations.

Jesus was not correcting the law of Moses—He was confronting those
who misused it. He addressed the religious leaders who exploited legal
loopholes for personal gain, using tradition to twist the intent of God's
commands. In doing so, He brought clarity and restoration to the law's
original purpose: love, justice, and mercy.

Don't Lust after a Woman was Already the Law

An example of understanding Jesus' teachings through the eyes of the
Jewish people would be Jesus' teachings on adultery. In Matthew 5, Jesus
makes a profound statement regarding the law of adultery.

Matthew 5:27-28 (KJV)
27. Ye have heard that it was said by them of old time, Thou shalt
not commit adultery:
28. But I say unto you, that whosoever looketh on a woman to lust
after her hath committed adultery with her already in his heart.

The law regarding adultery that Jesus quoted is found in Exodus 20:14 and Deuteronomy 5:18. According to JewishEncyclopedia.com, the crime of adultery according to the law of Moses is defined as "sexual intercourse of a married woman with any man other than her husband. The crime can be committed only by and with a married woman; for the unlawful intercourse of a married man with an unmarried woman is not technically Adultery in the Jewish law." We will explore later why this distinction was made—why a married man with an unmarried woman was not considered guilty of adultery under Israelite law.

By quoting the law pertaining to adultery, Jesus was clearly referring to married women in Matthew 5:27-28. The law of adultery did not apply to single, widowed, or divorced women. This interpretation was also common in other nations. Adultery was forbidden in Rome, Egypt, Mesopotamia, and even among the Philistines. For example, in Genesis 26, Abimelech, the king of the Philistines, questioned Isaac about his relationship with Rebekah. Although we have no surviving Philistine law code, it is more than likely that they based their cultural norms on Aegean honor-shame values and Canaanite assimilation, which would mean their punishment was possibly social (exile or retaliation) rather than formal legal punishment. Adultery was condemned in all these nations. Each of these nations had varying punishments for married women who committed adultery, as well as for the men involved.

In Matthew 5:27-28, Jesus first quotes the law of adultery, then explains, "Whoever looks at a woman with lust has already committed adultery with her in his heart." Many have taught that this was a new doctrine, but it was not. This teaching actually aligns with the law of Moses—specifically, the tenth commandment in the Ten Commandments, which forbids coveting another person's spouse.

Exodus 20:17 (KJV)
Thou shalt not covet thy neighbour's house, ***thou shalt not covet thy neighbour's wife***, nor his manservant, nor his maidservant, nor his ox, nor his ass, nor any thing that [is] thy neighbour's.

Deuteronomy 5:21 (KJV)
Neither shalt thou desire thy neighbour's wife, neither shalt thou covet thy neighbour's house, his field, or his manservant, or his maidservant, his ox, or his ass, or any [thing] that [is] thy neighbour's.

Paul explained that lusting is the sin of covetousness.

Romans 7:7 (KJV)
What shall we say then? [Is] the law sin? God forbid. Nay, I had not known sin, but by the law: for I had not known lust, except the law had said, Thou shalt not covet.

Jesus' teachings on lust are rooted in the law of Moses. Jesus did not introduce a new doctrine on adultery but reaffirmed the importance of obeying the Law of Moses. Given their Jewish background, Jesus' audience would have readily recognized the connection between His teachings and the Law of Moses.

THE LAWS OF MARRIAGE

To understand divorce within Israel, we must first understand the Jewish marriage process. This is especially important because every Jewish marriage required a form of prenup, which was part of the Jewish marriage contract. Additionally, much of Christian doctrine draws symbolic meaning from the structure of Jewish marriage, especially in reference to the relationship between Christ and the Church.

The Three Stages of Jewish Marriage

The marriage process in Judaism occurred in three distinct stages:

1. Shiddukhin – the promise or arrangement
2. Kiddushin – the legal betrothal
3. Nisuin – the final stage: "full fledged" marriage

Stage 1: *Shiddukhin* – The Promise

Shiddukhin refers to the initial arrangements before the legal betrothal. It was a mutual promise between a man and a woman to contract a marriage in the future. This agreement could be made directly by the individuals or arranged by their parents or relatives on their behalf. However, this stage did not legally change the couple's status.

Contrary to popular belief, a woman's consent was required. She could not be given in marriage without it. Jewish tradition upheld the principle of mutual consent. Rabbis teach mutual consent is supported by Deuteronomy 22:28–29, which deals with the case of a man having relations with a woman not betrothed. In such cases, implied consent is referenced, but it's also made clear that the man loses his right to divorce her if the father gave consent to the marriage (Exodus 22:17).

In Genesis 24 Abraham sent his servant to find a wife for his son Issac. Some teach Rebekah's consent to marry Isaac was an exception, but it wasn't. Rebekah and her family were approached, but what's often missed is the cultural significance of the gifts she received.

Genesis 24:22 (NIV)
When the camels had finished drinking, the man took out a gold nose ring weighing a beka and two gold bracelets weighing ten shekels.

Though the KJV refers to it as a "earring upon her face," the Hebrew and NIV states it was a nose ring—a customary betrothal gift in ancient Middle Eastern tradition. Bible scholars often refer to Ezekiel 16:12 as a confirmation of this symbolism.

Importantly, Rebekah gave her consent. Moses later made it law that daughters of Israel could not be married without their agreement.

According to The Jewish Betrothal (Kiddushin) Way in Love and Marriage by Maurice Lamm (Chabad.org):

"In Jewish law, taking a wife can never mean taking by force."

The Talmud expands on this, referencing Genesis 24:58, where Rebekah is asked directly whether she will go with Abraham's servant. Lamm notes:

"For marriage, the law requires daat— willing consent" as opposed to haskamah.

He further explains that the ring presented must have an easily determined value. If a woman were deceived—for example, believing a costume ring to be a diamond—she could legally rescind the marriage, as her consent would not have been informed or willing.

Stage 2: *Kiddushin* – The Betrothal

Kiddushin is the stage commonly translated as "betrothal," though it is much more serious than modern engagements. In Jewish law, Deuteronomy 24:1 refers directly to this stage:

Deuteronomy 24:1 (KJV)
When a man hath **taken a wife**, and married her...

At this point, the couple would sign the ketubah—a legally binding marriage contract. The ketubah outlined the man's responsibilities to the woman, including her dowry and a guaranteed sum she would receive in the event of death or divorce. In this way, it served as both a prenuptial agreement and a form of life insurance for the woman.

Once the ketubah was signed, the couple was considered legally married, though they had not yet consummated the marriage. A betrothal ceremony called erusin followed.

As part of their preparation, both the man and the woman would bathe in the mikvah, a ritual cleansing that symbolized spiritual purification before entering their covenant.

The ceremony began with a blessing over the wine, followed by the rabbi reciting the betrothal blessing (birkhat erusin). Next, the extension of the incest laws to include a mate's relatives was read, based on Leviticus 18 and 19. This made it clear that both partners' in-laws were now considered off-limits.

Then, a ring or token of value was given to the woman, and the man would say, "You are holy (m'kudesh or m'kudeshet) to me." In other words, the woman was now set apart—holy and dedicated exclusively to the man.

At this point, the couple was officially married, but the marriage was still incomplete. The woman was considered off-limits to all other men, including her husband, until the "full-fledged marriage" ceremony, known as nisuin. By signing the ketubah, the woman was legally married, but she could not fully fulfill her duties as a wife until the nisuin, which generally took place about a year later. In modern times, both the kiddushin and nisuin are often completed on the same day.

According to JewishEncyclopedia.com, when you search for "Betrothal in Talmudic Hebrew" by Marcus Jastrow and Bernard Drachman, it explains that after the betrothal, a period of twelve months was typically allowed to pass before the marriage was completed by the formal home-taking (nissu'in). In cases where the bride was a widow or the groom a widower, this interval was reduced to thirty days.

"In strict accordance with this sense, the rabbinical law declares that the betrothal is equivalent to an actual marriage and only to be dissolved by a formal divorce." At this point, if the couple decided to end their betrothal (engagement), the woman was required to receive a get (a bill of divorcement).

Christianity and Kiddushin

It is critical for Christians to understand the kiddushin stage of the Jewish marriage process, as the Church is currently in this stage. We are betrothed to Christ. To help illustrate this, I will highlight a portion of Christian doctrine to provide a clearer understanding.

2 Corinthians 11:2 (NKJV)
For I am jealous for you with godly jealousy. For I have betrothed
you to one husband, that I may present [you] [as] a chaste virgin to
Christ.

The Church is the bride of Christ, not yet the wife of Christ. Jesus referred to Himself as the Bridegroom, not the Husband. Likewise, John referred to himself as the friend—or best man—of the Bridegroom.

John 3:29 (NLT)
It is the bridegroom who marries the bride, and the best man is simply glad to stand with him and hear his vows. Therefore, I am filled with joy at his success.

When John the Baptist baptized Jesus, it marked Jesus' immersion into water—similar to the groom's ritual bath in the mikvah before the betrothal ceremony. The Jewish bride was required to immerse herself in water in the mikvah as part of the purification process for marriage. In the same way, the Church is called to be sanctified and cleansed, so that it may be presented to Christ without spot or wrinkle.

Ephesians 5:26-27 (KJV)
26. That he might sanctify and cleanse it with the washing of water by the word,
27. That he might present it to himself a glorious church, not having spot, or wrinkle, or any such thing; but that it should be holy and without blemish.

Kiddushin means holiness. There are several references Jesus made that indicate the Church is currently in the kiddushin stage of marriage. The Church is waiting for our Lord to return—for the marriage ceremony and the wedding feast to take place (Revelation 19:7, 9).

Matthew 25:1 (KJV)
Then shall the kingdom of heaven be likened unto ten virgins, which took their lamps, and went forth to meet the bridegroom.

The parable in Matthew 25 illustrates ten virgins. Virginity symbolizes purity. The virgins are betrothed and waiting for the return of the bridegroom, Jesus. This parable highlights the waiting period between the kiddushin and the nisuin.

"No man knows the day or the hour" is another Jewish reference to marriage made by Jesus, in which the father of the groom determined the time the bridegroom would come to retrieve his bride (Matthew 24:36). Similarly, "I go to prepare a place for you" is a reference to kiddushin—the betrothal phase of a Jewish marriage—in which the groom would go away to prepare the bride's chamber while the bride awaited his return (John 14:2).

Stage 3: The *Nisuin* (The Full-Fledged Marriage)

Deuteronomy 24:1 (KJV)
When a man hath taken a wife, ***and married*** her...

The full-fledged wedding is called a nisuin (or nissuin). The ceremony begins with the veiling ritual known as bedeken, which is performed by the husband or a rabbi. This tradition is meant to prevent the kind of mistake Jacob made when he unknowingly married Leah instead of Rachel (Genesis 24:60). During this ceremony, the bride's hair is veiled for the remainder of her life, following the example set by Rebekah, who veiled herself upon meeting Isaac (Genesis 24:65). Today, a married Jewish woman typically wears a head covering or a wig.

The vows are exchanged under the chuppah. This exchange differs from secular weddings. Since the bride has already signed the ketubah, she has formally consented to be his wife. Therefore, the bridegroom alone makes the verbal declaration: "Harei at mekudeshet li"—"You are consecrated to me in accordance with the law of Moshe (Moses) and Israel." The ketubah (marriage agreement) is then read aloud to the guests in Aramaic. The couple blesses the wine and recites the seven benedictions (sheva brachot). After the ceremony, the couple enters the yichud—the "seclusion room"—where they are alone together for the first time.

THE LAW OF DIVORCE

The law regarding divorce is found in Deuteronomy 24:1-4. The law states that for a marriage to be dissolved, the man is required to give the woman a bill of divorcement, known as a get (or gett). This process is called the get ceremony. The ceremony takes place in a tribunal court (Beit Din – Deuteronomy 16:18), which handles all civil cases. It is overseen by three judges, all of whom are experts on divorce, with at least one of them being required to be a rabbi.

The get is drafted by a scribe on behalf of the man. The man must place the get in the woman's hand, after which she is sent away from his house. This must be done in the presence of two witnesses. Once the woman receives the get, she is free to marry another man.

Additionally, the law states that if the woman is divorced a second time or if her second husband dies, she is not permitted to return to her first husband. However, she may marry a third husband. Jewish tradition teaches that a marriage ends in two ways: by death or by divorce, as stated in Deuteronomy 24:3.

Deuteronomy 24:1-4 (NLT)
1. "Suppose a man marries a woman but she does not please him. Having discovered something wrong with her, he writes her a letter of divorce, hands it to her, and sends her away from his house.
2. When she leaves his house, she is free to marry another man.
3. But if the second husband also turns against her and *divorces* her, *or* if he *dies*,

4. the first husband may not marry her again, for she has been defiled. That would be detestable to the LORD. You must not bring guilt upon the land the LORD your God is giving you as a special possession.

The man could take his wife back as long as she had not married another man. However, the woman became defiled to her former husband once she married and consummated her second marriage.

Jesus' Teachings on Divorce Can't Violate the Law

Matthew 5:31-32 (KJV)
31. It hath been said, whosoever shall put away his wife, let him give her a writing of divorcement:
32. But I say unto you, that whosoever shall put away his wife, saving for the cause of fornication, causeth her to commit adultery: and whosoever shall marry her that is divorced committeth adultery.

Matthew 19:9 (KJV)
And I say unto you, whosoever shall put away his wife, except [it be] for fornication, and shall marry another, committeth adultery: and whoso marrieth her which is put away doth commit adultery.

Mark 10:11-12 (KJV)
11. And he saith unto them, whosoever shall put away his wife, and marry another, committeth adultery against her.
12. And if a woman shall put away her husband, and be married to another, she committeth adultery.

The conclusion drawn from Jesus' teachings is that divorce is no longer permitted for any cause. The only just cause for divorce, according to many interpretations of Jesus' words, is adultery. However, Jesus did not explicitly use the word "adultery." Those familiar with the Greek language know that Jesus used the term porneia (fornication) rather than moichaō (adultery). This distinction has sparked debates regarding Jesus' reasoning for choosing this specific word. Some argue that Jesus' statements may have been directed at the betrothal period rather than the actual marriage, concluding Jesus restricted divorce to the betrothal period.

Some scholars point to the debates between Sage Hillel and Sage Shammai, who founded two distinct schools of thought within Judaism. These schools often disagreed on various aspects of family law, including divorce. Some argue that Jesus was asked to weigh in on their differences, offering His own interpretation of the law.

However, there is a major issue with these interpretations: they all violate the law of Moses. Jesus explicitly stated that He did not come to abolish the law (Matthew 5:17). Therefore, teachings suggesting that Jesus was altering or changing the law regarding divorce would inherently contradict His own declaration and imply that He sought to change the law of Moses in some way.

Matthew 5:17 (KJV)
Think not that I am come to destroy the law, or the prophets: I am
not come to destroy, but to fulfil.

There are no examples in the Scriptures where the scribes, Sadducees, or Pharisees accused Jesus of changing, violating, or abolishing the law of Moses. On many occasions, they tried to trap Jesus in debates to bring charges against Him. Despite their legal arguments and attempts, Jesus left them in silence as He made His responses. All of Jesus' answers to His opponents were rooted in the law of Moses, often quoting it directly in His defense. The charges brought against Jesus were based on His declaration that He would destroy the Temple of God and rebuild it in three days, as mentioned during His trial in Matthew 26. However, His accusers were unable to provide any proof that He had taught anything contrary to the law of Moses.

Jesus' statements were conclusive truths that did not violate or alter the law of Moses. In fact, they addressed growing trends in Israel that were violations of the law. So, let's first examine the law of adultery and the law of fornication to gain a clearer understanding of how the law of Moses interpreted these offenses.

THE LAW OF ADULTERY

Adultery is a crime. In Israel, the word "sin" was synonymous with "crime." A person who committed a sin in Israel understood they were committing a crime and could be punished according to the law of Moses.

Most Christians do not view adultery as a crime today. However, adultery was and still is considered a crime in the United States, although it is no longer enforced in many states. In the past, the penalty for adultery included fines, jail time, and, in some states, it was even considered a felony.

In Israel, adultery was a capital crime that was punishable by death.

Deuteronomy 22:22 (KJV)
If a man be found lying with a woman married to an husband,
then they shall both of them die, [both] the man that lay with the
woman, and the woman: so shalt thou put away evil from Israel.

Leviticus 20:10 (KJV)
And the man that committeth adultery with [another] man's wife,
[even he] that committeth adultery with his neighbour's wife, the
adulterer and the adulteress shall surely be put to death.

Adultery was a capital crime. Both the married woman and the man involved were to be put to death. The Jewish Encyclopedia defines adultery as "sexual intercourse of a married woman with any man other than her husband. The crime can be committed only by and with a married woman; for the unlawful intercourse of a married man with an unmarried woman is not technically adultery in Jewish law."

A married man could only be charged with adultery if the woman he was with was a married woman. If the married man was with an unmarried woman (whether single, divorced, or widowed), then the law did not apply.

Polygamy

A married man with an unmarried woman (whether single, divorced, or widowed) was not viewed as committing the crime of adultery because men could have multiple wives in Israel, as seen in Exodus 21:10. While polygamy was permitted, it was not common because it was expensive. The most common reasons for polygamy included barrenness. Couples who did not want to divorce but wanted to have children could opt for polygamy.

For a man to take an additional wife, the consent of the first wife was required. Tractate Yevamot 65a explains that if the first wife did not approve, she had the right to demand a divorce; the husband was then obligated to grant the divorce and pay her the full amount of her ketubah (marriage contract). The Talmud refers to a co-wife as a "tzarah," a term related to the Hebrew root for "trouble," reflecting the potential difficulties such a situation could cause.

Rival Wives

A man could not house both wives together to prevent tsârâh ("female rival"). The man was required to provide a home for each of his wives. The reasoning is both practical and moral: cohabiting two wives in the same residence could lead to jealousy, conflict, and emotional harm, which Judaism sought to prevent.

Jewish law prohibited a man from marrying two sisters simultaneously. This regulation was intended to prevent familial conflict, as exemplified in the tension between Leah and Rachel in the Torah.

Leviticus 18:18 (KJV)
Neither shalt thou take a wife to her sister, to vex her, to uncover
her nakedness, beside the other in her life time.

This prohibition only applies to concurrent marriages. Once the wife died the man was permitted to marry his wife's sister after the first wife had died. Some rabbinic interpretations allowed marriage to a former wife's sister after a valid divorce, since the sisters would no longer be co-wives.

The Problem with Polygamy

Though polygamy was lawful in Israel, polyandry was unlawful. Under Jewish law, a woman can never be married to more than one man at the same time. Any second union before a valid get is not considered marriage at all but adultery (eshet ish), one of the gravest prohibitions in the Torah. Even the suspicion of a second husband without a divorce renders the second union invalid and adulterous. However, men were allowed to remarry without the need of a get (bill of divorcement), whereas women were required to present a bill of divorcement to the priest to remarry. Under the Law of Moses (Torah), a man was never commanded to give or receive a get in order to remarry. The requirement of a get applies only to the woman. This law was a key factor in the loophole created in the law of Moses, directly responsible for the agunah crisis.

THE LAWS OF FORNICATION

Fornication is commonly defined within Christian communities as sex outside of wedlock. However, in Jewish culture, there is no single "all-purpose" Hebrew word that directly means "sex outside of marriage." Instead, different terms are used depending on the circumstance – such as na'af (adultery) for relations involving a married person, or zenut (sexual immorality, often linked with prostitution or promiscuity). In Jewish law, a child is not automatically considered mamzer (bastard) simply because he or she was born to unmarried parents. The term mamzer applies to offspring from an adulterous union or incestuous union, not an unwed union. If a single Jewish woman has sex with a single Jewish man, the child is considered fully Jewish and legitimate in the community. If the woman is Jewish and the man is a non-Jew then the child is considered fully Jewish. Jewishness follows the mother, per Mishnah Kiddushin 3:12. However, if the man is Jewish and the woman is non-Jewish the child is not Jewish. According to Halakha, that child would be considered a Gentile unless they undergo proper conversion. In both cases the child is not a mamzer.

The English word "fornication" was borrowed into Middle English through Anglo-French in the 14th century. Over time it came to mean sexual relations between two unmarried persons, which is how many Christians understand it today.

By contrast, Jewish law approaches the matter not through a single term, but through the structure of laws and boundaries. These laws would include the law of negiah and the law of yichud.

The Law of Touch (*Negiah*)

In Israel, the law of touch (negiah) was practiced by all Jews. Men and women were forbidden from touching someone of the opposite sex unless they were married to them. As a result, married couples did not—and still do not—engage in open displays of affection.

The Law of Seclusion (*Yichud*)

Women were forbidden from being secluded with a man they were not married to, including men of certain degrees of kinship. This law prevented any situation where a woman and a man could be alone together in private, which could lead to inappropriate behavior.

Jews practice shomer negiah, which means refraining from physical contact with the opposite sex until marriage. A shomer (guardian) is often present during dating to prevent situations of yichud (seclusion).

These customs and practices are based on Leviticus 18:6, which includes laws concerning incest and appropriate boundaries between men and women.

Leviticus 18:6 (KJV)
None of you shall approach to any that is near of kin to him, to uncover [their] nakedness: I [am] the LORD.

Additionally, all men were required to bathe (ceremonially) in a mikvah for spiritual purity and to remove uncleanness. Men could not bring an offering to God or visit the temple without first being purified in the mikvah. Men would bathe in the mikvah every Sabbath. In addition to this, the mikvah was used for other significant life events such as births, deaths, marriage, and divorce. It is recommended to look up the mikvah for a deeper understanding of its significance and usage in Jewish tradition.

Leviticus 11:36 (KJV)
Nevertheless a fountain or pit, [wherein there is] plenty
(Translation: miqvê Pronunciation: mik-veh') of water, shall be
clean: but that which toucheth their carcase shall be unclean.

Only married and betrothed women went to the mikvah when they became tamei (spiritually impure). All other women (single, divorced, and widowed) were forbidden from using the mikvah and were thus considered to be in a constant state of niddah. Niddah refers to the period when a woman is menstruating. During this time, according to Jewish law, a woman is spiritually impure. For this reason, Jewish men viewed women as "unclean," as single, divorced, and widowed women were seen as being in a continuous state of niddah.

The mikvah was required for both men and women (betrothed and married) for ceremonial cleanliness, not bodily cleanliness, similar to the concept of Christian baptism. Because of this, men would not touch women who were not their wives, as this would spiritually defile them. This law also applied to married men touching their wives during the period of niddah, which would make the man unclean (Leviticus 15:19), or women who had recently given birth (Leviticus 12).

As a rabbi explained to me, a man touching a woman who was not his wife was considered a highly shameful act. It brought dishonor to his family, and the community would view him as weak. Virginity and modesty were highly valued qualities in women.

A woman who secretly lost her virginity but presented herself as a virgin at the time of marriage could face death. Her status as a virgin, married, or widowed was recorded on the marriage contract and determined the bride price (Exodus 22:17). Lying about her virginity could result in severe consequences. Once a woman was betrothed, committing fornication was punished as severely as adultery.

Deuteronomy 22:20-21 (KJV)
20. But if this thing be true, [and the tokens of] virginity be not found for the damsel:
21. Then they shall bring out the damsel to the door of her father's house, and the men of her city shall stone her with stones that she die: because she hath wrought folly in Israel, to play the whore in her father's house: so shalt thou put evil away from among you.

The Prenup (The *Ketubah*)

A woman's status—whether virgin, widow, or divorcee—was documented in her marriage contract, known as the ketubah. The ketubah served as protection for the woman, outlining the husband's obligations to her (such as food, clothing, and conjugal rights as per Exodus 21:10), the woman's dowry, and what she would receive financially if the man divorced her or passed away. In essence, every Jewish marriage had a marriage contract that required a "prenuptial agreement" and "life insurance" be included.

It was customary for the ketubah payment (divorce settlement) to be equal to the woman's dowry. However, the law set a minimum amount that had to be paid. This minimum obligation, known as the ikkar ketubah, was 200 silver denarii for a virgin bride and 100 silver denarii for a widow or divorced woman (Exodus 22:17). The purpose was to ensure that the woman would have at least a year's worth of living expenses.

The law of Moses required every Israelite woman to have a dowry. According to jewishvirtuallibrary.com, the community funds provided the dowry for an orphan or a very poor girl. "In case of her father's death, the brothers of a minor girl were obliged to give her the minimum dowry, and the court estimated how much her father would have given her above the minimum dowry. The sum was then taken out of the father's estate and given to the daughter upon majority (Ket. 6:6; 68a–69b). In the absence of such an estimate, each daughter was entitled to receive one-tenth of the value of her father's estate in money or valuables (Yad, Ishut, 20:4–7; Sh. Ar., EH 113:4). If the father was unable or unwilling to pay the promised dowry at the betrothal ceremony, the groom could refuse to marry his bride (Ket. 13:5; Ket. 108b–109a). Insistence on exact payment of the promised dowry, however, was frowned upon by later rabbinic authorities (Rema to Sh. Ar., EH 2:1)."

The Bride Price (*Mohar*)

The man paid a bride price, called a mohar, to the woman's father (Exodus 22:17). This amount varied based on the woman's status—whether she was a virgin, divorced, or widowed. Therefore, the woman could not falsify her ketubah by claiming she was a virgin if she was not.

The bride price was viewed as a gift, not a purchase of the bride. If the man had the right to purchase his bride, it would imply that he could also sell her, which was unlawful in Israel.

The Limitations for Priests (*Chalal* and *Chalalah*)

Only priests were forbidden from marrying divorced women, widows, or harlots, as stated in Leviticus 21:7. This law applied specifically to the tribe of Levi. Marrying a woman from one of these categories was not a crime punishable by death; however, children born of such a union would carry the status of chalal (male) or chalalah (female), disqualifying them from the priesthood and priestly duties.

While the marriage persisted, the priest also could not serve in the Temple or perform priestly rites. To remove the spiritual and ritual violation, the kohen had to divorce the forbidden wife. A get would end the marriage, allowing the priest to marry a woman he was permitted to marry and preserve the priestly lineage.

If a priest's daughter was caught playing the harlot, the law required her to be burned to death.

Leviticus 21:9 (NLT)
"If a priest's daughter defiles herself by becoming a prostitute, she also defiles her father's holiness, and she must be burned to death."

FORBIDDEN MARRIAGES

As citizens of the nation of Israel, there were several forbidden marriages according to the law. Maurice Lamm's article, Prohibited Marriages (published on Chabad.com), outlines these restrictions. He provides four lists: "A Man May Not Marry," "A Man May Marry," "A Woman May Not Marry," and "A Woman May Marry." These lists differ for men and women.

Below, I've combined and summarized several of these lists to highlight the forbidden marriages in Israel:

Forbidden Marriages in Israel

1. Anyone not Jewish: Jews were forbidden from marrying non-Jews, based on Deuteronomy 7:3.
2. The daughter/son of an adulterous or incestuous union: Marriage with a child born of an adulterous or incestuous relationship was prohibited.
3. A married woman or man, until the civil and Jewish divorces have been completed: A married person could not marry someone else until both civil and Jewish divorces were fully finalized.
4. His own divorced wife after her remarriage to another man and the latter's death or divorce: A man could not remarry his own divorced wife after she had married another man and that second marriage ended in either death or divorce.

5. A married woman with whom he committed adultery, but now is divorced or widowed: A man could not marry a woman with whom he had committed adultery, even if she was now divorced or widowed.

6. A kohen (priest) may not marry:
   o A divorced woman
   o A chalutzah (widow)
   o A convert (to Judaism)
   o A zonah (prostitute)
   o A chalalah (a woman disqualified from the priesthood due to her birth status)

Explanation of Forbidden Marriages

1. Restrictions on Marrying Non-Jews:

Deuteronomy 7:3 (KJV)
Neither shalt thou make marriages with them;
thy daughter thou shalt not give unto his son, nor his daughter
shalt thou take unto thy son.

Jews could marry non-Jews if they converted to Judaism. The conversion process is done through the Beit Din (the Jewish tribunal court) as outlined in Leviticus 19:34. A convert is fully accepted into the Jewish community and is not distinguished from those born into the faith.

Deuteronomy 7:1-2 lists seven nations, and Deuteronomy 23:8-9 lists two nations that Israelites were not permitted to marry. Interestingly, the Egyptians and the Philistines are not on this list. While many teach that Samson's marriage to the Philistine woman violated the law of Moses, it's worth noting that Samson's wife never converted. If marriage to a non-Jewish person was completely unlawful, then Ruth and Rahab's marriages would have been considered invalid. However, both Ruth's marriage to

Boaz (Booz) and Rahab's marriage to Salmon (Matthew 1:5, Luke 3:32) birthed the bloodline of Jesus. Both Ruth and Rahab converted to the faith, forsaking their gods and embracing the God of Israel.

Additionally, there were Egyptians who left Egypt with the Israelites (Exodus 12:38) and a group of Midianites known as the Kenites, who lived among the Israelites. The Kenites first encountered the Hebrews at Mount Sinai, and Moses himself was married to a Kenite. His father-in-law, Jethro (also known as Reuel or Raguel), was a Midianite priest. Moses even asked Hobab, his brother-in-law, to help guide the Israelites through the wilderness because he knew the terrain well (Numbers 10:29-32). The Kenites eventually became scribes and teachers of the law of Moses (Judges 1:16, 1 Chronicles 2:55, Jeremiah 35—the house of the Rechabites). The Kenites even had their own cities within Israel (1 Samuel 27:10).

2. The Daughter/Son of an Adulterous or Incestuous Union

A Jew could not marry the daughter or son of an adulterous or incestuous union. Children born from such unions were classified as *mamzer* (male) and *mamzeret* (female). According to Jewish law, a mamzer could only marry another mamzeret, and vice versa.

Deuteronomy 23:2 (KJV)
A bastard (mamzēr) shall not enter into the congregation of the LORD; even to his tenth generation shall he not enter into the congregation of the LORD.

We will examine the mamzer and mamzeret in further detail shortly. Understanding this law is critical to understanding Jesus' teachings.

3. A married woman or man, until the civil and Jewish divorces have been completed.

A couple whose divorce is not yet complete is still considered married. Only after the divorce is finalized can the woman enter into another marriage.

Deuteronomy 24:3-4 (KJV)
1. When a man hath taken a wife, and married her,
and it come to pass that she find no favour in his eyes,
because he hath found some uncleanness in her: then let him write
her a bill of divorcement, and give it in her hand, and send her out
of his house.
2. And when she is departed out of his house, she may go and
be another man's wife.

4. His own divorced wife after her remarriage to another man and the latter's death or divorce.

This law is explained in Deuteronomy 24:3. If the woman's second husband dies or divorces her, she is not permitted to return to her first husband.

Deuteronomy 24:3-4 (NLT)
3 But if the second husband also turns against her and divorces her,
or if he dies,
4 then her first husband, who divorced her, is not allowed to marry
her again after she has been defiled. That would be detestable in
the eyes of the LORD. Do not bring sin upon the land the LORD
your God is giving you as an inheritance.

5. A married woman with whom he committed adultery, but now is divorced or widowed.

If a husband suspected infidelity, the woman was forbidden from the accused man forever. This rule applied even after her husband died, and even if the (accused) man were to become divorced or widowed.

The law of Moses outlined how infidelity was to be handled. The law of sotah (or sota), also called the law of jealousy, is found in Numbers 5.

Numbers 5:29 (KJV)
This [is] the law of jealousies, when a wife goeth aside [to another] instead of her husband, and is defiled;

Numbers 5:12 (KJV)
Speak unto the children of Israel, and say unto them, If any man's wife go aside {śāṭâ}, and commit a trespass against him

There was a ritual the priests were required to follow that involved the woman taking an oath and the drinking of bitter water. For the woman to undergo the ritual, the husband must first have warned the wife about secluding herself with the suspected man in the presence of two witnesses. Then, if the woman is subsequently seen by two witnesses engaging in certain promiscuous behavior, only then can the woman be brought to the temple.

This law also applied to a man who found himself in an adulterous marriage (married to a woman who was still legally married to her first husband). He would be off-limits to the woman forever. We will examine adulterous marriages in more detail in a little bit.

6. A kohen (priest) may not marry a divorced woman, a chalutzah (widow), a convert (to Judaism), a zonah (prostitute), or a chalalah.

This law only applied to the kohen (priest). Men from all the other tribes did not have these limitations. A priest could not marry divorced women, widows, converts, harlots, or women (chalalah) disqualified from the priesthood. A chalalah was a woman born from a marriage between a priest and a widow, divorced woman, convert, or harlot. In Leviticus 21:14, a chalalah would be considered "profane."

Leviticus 21:13-14 (KJV)
13. And he shall take a wife in her virginity.
14. A widow, or a divorced woman, or *profane*, [or] an harlot, these shall he not take: but he shall take a virgin of his own people to wife.

THE BASTARD (*MAMZER*)

Adulterous Marriages and Incestuous Marriages

On the list of forbidden marriages, we see that a Jew could not marry a mamzer or mamzeret.

According to American and English definitions, a bastard is a child born to unmarried (unwed) parents, an illegitimate child. This is not the case in Israel, and this is the reason Christian teachings on the subject are erroneous. There is no equivalent word in Hebrew for "bastard."

In Israel, any child born to an unwed mother is simply a Jew. According to Jewish tradition, a person's Jewish heritage is determined by their mother. So, if a person's mother is Jewish, they are considered Jewish regardless of their father's religious background. This practice is called matrilineal descent. We can see an example of this in the scriptures, where Paul praises Timothy's mother and grandmother (2 Timothy 1:5), with his father being Greek (Acts 16:1, 3).

On the other hand, a mamzer is an illegitimate child, but not because the parents were unwed. The status of mamzer was given to a child born out of an incestuous or adulterous marriage. These were children born to wedded parents whose marriages were later deemed unlawful.

Jewishencyclopedia.com defines a mamzer as "the offspring of a father and mother between whom there could be in law no binding betrothal." This means that the marriage agreement (the ketubah), which was drafted by the scribe and signed by two witnesses, was later deemed by the court to be illegitimate and non-binding. The law for an adulterous marriage is not the same as the law of adultery. The law of an adulterous marriage can be found in Deuteronomy 23:2.

Deuteronomy 23:2 (KJV)
A mamzer shall not enter the assembly of the LORD; even to the tenth generation none of his descendants shall enter.

An Incestuous Marriage

An incestuous marriage was a marriage between a bride and groom who were too closely related. These relationships are listed in Leviticus 18:6-18. This was one of the laws John the Baptist referenced when he stated that King Herod's marriage was unlawful.

Mark 6:18 (KJV) For John had said unto Herod, It is not lawful for thee to have thy brother's wife.

An Adulterous Marriage

Christians teach that an adulterous marriage is a marriage following a divorce. However, this is not true in any country except within Christian culture, and it is a fallacy.

In Israel, once a woman received her get (bill of divorcement), she was free to marry another man. Jewish law does not allow a divorced woman without a get to remarry. The divorced woman had to present her bill of divorce (get) to the priest in order to remarry.

Isaiah 50:1 (KJV) Thus saith the LORD, Where [is] the bill of your mother's divorcement, whom I have put away?

So how was it possible for a child to be born in adultery,
a union between a married woman and a man other than
her husband?

If the man was missing due to being captured in battle or even abandonment, the woman was not permitted to remarry. She took on the status agunah, which is Hebrew for "anchored" or "chained." Agunah or aginut is derived from the word agan found in Ruth 1:13. The bill of divorcement had to be placed into the woman's hand by the man. This was not possible in his absence. To avoid this problem Moses required men to give their wives a conditional divorce before leaving for battle. However, there were many times when men would go off to do business and never returned home. In ancient Israel, it was common for married couples to live apart for extended periods – something we also observe in the lives of Jesus' disciples, who often traveled with Him while leaving their families at home.

An adulterous marriage would only occur in Israel if the woman entered a bigamous marriage inadvertently (or at times purposely). For example, if the woman was "incorrectly" informed by two witnesses of her legal husband's death, she would then be free to remarry. If it was later discovered that the woman's husband was still living, her second marriage was deemed invalid. The general principle is that "a woman cannot be the wife of two [men]." While the woman's first marriage subsists, a purported marriage to another man is thus totally invalid. Therefore, the second marriage was deemed adulterous, and the man (second "husband") would receive the status of adulterer.

The witnesses were required to have witnessed the death of the husband or his funeral. The witness or witnesses were also prohibited from marrying the woman. The same applied to witnesses who had signed the get (bill of divorcement) during the get ceremony.

To fix the issue of an adulterous marriage, the court required the woman to be divorced from her first husband, though she was rendered prohibited to him (Deuteronomy 24:4). She was required to be divorced from her adulterous "husband" even though the court viewed the second marriage as invalid. She would lose her **ketubah** from both men, but she was entitled to her dowry. Any children from the invalid marriage were classified as mamzer (bastards). The woman would then be prohibited from remarrying either man forever, even if one of them died. However, she would be free to marry another man.

If a divorced couple chose to remarry, that was permitted by law. Hachzarat grushato is a Hebrew phrase that literally means "the return of his divorced wife" or "taking back his ex-wife." A man may divorce his wife and later remarry her only if she has not married someone else in the meantime. If she did marry another man and was then divorced or widowed, her first husband is forbidden to remarry her.

In Jewish law (halakha), after a divorce, a Jewish woman was required to wait a minimum of three months before remarrying. This waiting period is based on a rabbinic decree found in the Talmud (Yevamot 41a), established to prevent confusion over paternity in case the woman was pregnant from her first husband. If the woman was clearly not pregnant (e.g., elderly or post-menopausal), some authorities might permit a shorter waiting period. In certain urgent cases (like yibbum - levirate marriage), rabbinic courts could make case-by-case decisions. Men did not have to wait any period before remarrying.

Under Jewish law, the waiting period, known as the "waiting period after divorce," is intended to ensure that any potential pregnancy from the previous marriage can be identified, thus avoiding any uncertainty about the paternity of a child. Uncertainty regarding paternity would create issues regarding inheritance and child support (in modern times). Even though now the paternity of a child can be determined through DNA, the court still adheres to the law. This civil law was based on an old notion of pregnancy lengths, even though modern medicine shows this is outdated. This notion was not based on modern medical understanding but rather legal and moral caution – to avoid disputes over paternity and protect inheritance rights or marital legitimacy.

The news article "Father unknown': A dread biblical status leads to modern problems" by Judah Ari Gross, Times of Israel, April 14, 2022, shares the story of a man whose child was born in Israel less than 300 days after her mother's divorce from another man. The law in Israel lists any child born within 300 days of their mother's divorce be officially listed as the offspring of their mother's ex-husband, with the average pregnancy being 280 days (40 weeks). The man has been fighting to have his name listed officially as his daughter's father and also to have the status of mamzer removed from his daughter's name.

To learn more, search "Bigamy and Polygamy" at jewishvirtuallibrary. com, "Divorce" at jewfaq.org, or "Illegitimacy" at jewishencyclopedia. com.

Mamzer List (Backlist) - *Reshimat Mamzerim*

If someone is suspected of being a mamzer (due to parentage or irregularities in divorce/remarriage), their status may be flagged by the rabbinical court when they try to marry. A mamzer list (also called a "blacklist" or in Hebrew, reshimat mamzerim) is an unofficial or confidential list maintained by some rabbinical courts (batei din) that tracks individuals who are suspected or confirmed to have mamzer status under halakha (Jewish law). Rabbinical authorities might then block the marriage until the person's status is clarified. Such individuals are prohibited from marrying into the broader Jewish community, except other mamzerim or converts (in some interpretations). These lists are still maintained today and have been challenged legally in court. In 2014, the Center for Women's Justice petitioned the Israeli Supreme Court to bar secret blacklists of mamzerim by rabbinical courts, on the grounds of invasion of privacy. The woman who petitioned the court was one of more than 5,000 Israelis included on a list of people restricted from marrying based on prohibitions in traditional Jewish law. To learn more about the case, look up "Barring 'bastards': Israel's marriage blacklist said to break privacy laws," by Ben Sales, Times of Israel, May 7, 2014.

Child Custody

Before we look at Jesus' teachings on divorce, another important area to address is how child custody was handled. While many teach that the woman received custody of the children following the divorce, this is American law and customs, not the case in Israel. After the divorce, the woman would generally return to her father's home (Leviticus 22:13). She would leave her children with her former husband. Jewishvirtuallibrary.com, in their article on divorce, quotes Ket. 65b: "Special arrangements were probably made for sucking infants; in later law, boys, at least, had to be returned to their father's home by the time they were six years old."

JESUS' TEACHINGS ON DIVORCE

Let's look again at Jesus' teachings on divorce and see if they in fact align with the law of Moses or if they contradict the law as so many have taught.

Matthew 5:31-32 (KJV)
31. It hath been said, Whosoever shall put away his wife, let him give her a writing of divorcement:
32. But I say unto you, That whosoever shall put away his wife, saving for the cause of fornication, causeth her to commit adultery: and whosoever shall marry her that is divorced committeth adultery.

In Matthew 5:31, Jesus begins by quoting the law of Moses. This is the law of divorce found in Deuteronomy 24:1-4. Jesus states that whoever sends his wife away must give her a bill of divorcement. This coincides with the law as stated in Deuteronomy 24. The man was to give the woman the bill of divorce and then send her out of his house.

Deuteronomy 24:1 (KJV)
...then let him write her a bill of divorcement, and give [it] in her hand, and send her out of his house.

There were three required parts to the divorce proceedings: the get (bill of divorcement), the man must place it in the woman's hand, and she is to be sent away. Jesus mentions two of these parts in Matthew 5:31.

Matthew 5:31
It hath been said, Whosoever shall <u>put away his wife</u> [**apolyo**], let him <u>give her a writing of divorcement</u> [**apostasion**]:

"Put away" is the Greek word apolyō, which means: to set free, to let go, dismiss, bid to depart, release. "Writing of divorcement" is the Greek word apostasion, which means: divorce, repudiation. Notice the Greek words in verse 32. Jesus never stated that "whosoever shall put away his wife <u>and</u> give her a writing of divorcement, whosoever shall marry her committeth adultery."

Matthew 5:32
But I say unto you, That whosoever shall put away [**apolyō**] his wife, saving for the cause of fornication, causeth her to commit adultery: and whosoever shall marry her that is divorced [**apolyō**] committeth adultery.

We do not find the word apostasion used at all in Matthew 5:32. Jesus said, "Whosoever shall marry her that is apolyō [dismissed, released, sent away] commits adultery." A woman who is dismissed is a woman who has not yet received her get (bill of divorcement). Jesus is describing a couple that is separated, not a couple that is legally divorced.

The law of Moses forbade the divorcing of a wife by words only. Such a divorce was not permitted or viewed as valid by the court. However, the dismissal of a concubine was legal because she did not have a **ketubah**. No formal divorce was required in that case. Some church circles have taught that Israelite men would divorce their wives by writing on paper, "I divorce you," three times. This was not an Israelite practice; it is a reference to triple talaq, a controversial Islamic practice that allows Muslim men to divorce their wives by saying the Arabic word for divorce, talaq, three times. This was not a custom practiced in Israel.

Jesus' teaching that a person who enters a second marriage while only being separated from their spouse and not legally divorced is committing adultery aligns with the third forbidden marriage: "A married woman or man, until the civil and Jewish divorces have been completed." If a couple were to marry before the divorce to a former spouse was complete, such a marriage would be classed by the Jewish court as an adulterous marriage. The woman would be considered an adulteress, and the man who married her would be considered an adulterer. This was not a capital crime, unlike the crime of adultery. The penalty for an adulterous marriage was mandatory divorce from both the first and second "adulterer" husbands. The woman must receive a get from both men. She would forfeit her ketubah from both men. Any children from the adulterous marriage would be classified as mamzer or mamzeret. She would be forbidden from both men forever, no matter the circumstances.

As we examine all of Jesus' statements, we will find him referencing this law (Deuteronomy 24:1-4). This law states that only after the woman has received her bill of divorcement, she could be another man's wife. A woman could not remarry while she was only "put away". The divorce had to be final.

Matthew 19:9 (KJV)
And I say unto you, Whosoever shall put away [apolyō] his wife, except [it be] for fornication, and shall marry another, committeth adultery: and whoso marrieth her which is put away [apolyō] doth commit adultery.

Mark 10:11-12 (KJV)
11. And he saith unto them, Whosoever shall put away [apolyō] his wife, and marry another, committeth adultery against her.
12. And if a woman shall put away [apolyō] her husband, and be married to another, she committeth adultery.

Jesus was not talking about marriages following a divorce. Jesus was talking about remarrying while the first marriage was still legally binding.

Can we find this forbidden marriage in the law of Moses? Yes!

Children produced in this type of unlawful union, which would be an adulterous marriage (or even an incestuous union), would have the status of mamzer or bastard. The law is found in Deuteronomy 23:2.

Deuteronomy 23:2 (KJV)
A bastard [mamzer] shall not enter into the congregation of the LORD; even to his tenth generation shall he not enter into the congregation of the LORD.

An Adulterous Marriage In The Bible (Michal and Philti)

We can find an example of an adulterous marriage in the scriptures. In this example, we can see the law of Moses being enforced.

In 1 Samuel 18:27, David married King Saul's daughter Michal. In 1 Samuel 19, Saul sent men to kill David, and David escaped through a window. David was then on the run from Saul for many years. During that time, Saul gave Michal to another man to marry (1 Samuel 25:44). Michal's marriage to Philti (also called Phaltiel) was technically an unlawful "adulterous marriage." When David returned, he demanded of Michal's brother, Ishbosheth, that Michal be returned to him.

2 Samuel 3:15 (KJV)
"And Ishbosheth sent, and took her from [her] husband, [even] from Phaltiel the son of Laish."

David's marriage to Michal was still binding, though he had been gone for many years. Michal was agunah. By law, Michal's second marriage would have been labeled an adulterous marriage. Once David returned, by law, he should have been required to divorce Michal because she was now defiled to him. However, there is a part of this story that many Christians are unfamiliar with. Christians have recounted this story with many errors, often applying American laws, culture, and romance to it. We must apply Jewish laws and culture.

First, Philti never consummated his marriage with Michal. He knew that to do so would have been committing adultery. This would not have been considered adultery because they would have had a marriage agreement. However, the question remained about David's status—was he alive or dead? David was not dead, and Michal did not have a get from David. So, Philti placed a sword in the bed between them, and he and Michal vowed to take their lives if they crossed the sword. If David were to die in battle, then she would be free to be Philti's wife. However, David did not die, and he returned home.

This is why Philti cried in 2 Samuel 3:16, because David's return meant his act of righteousness (keeping the law and not touching another man's wife) proved futile. Philti is later called Phaltiel because his name was changed. The Jewish rabbis teach, "He was given the name Paltiel (palat-el) because God (El) attests of him that he was saved (niflat) from sin and did not touch David's wife (Lev. Rabbah 23:10)."

Michal was required by law to return to David. Phaltiel was praised for his righteousness and was mentioned in Proverbs 31 in the proverb from the mother of King Lemuel about the virtuous woman. The rabbis teach that Phaltiel had to take on the mindset of a woman to refrain from touching Michal.

Proverbs 31:29 (KJV)
Many daughters have done virtuously, but thou excellest them all.

Another part of Michal's story that Christians get grossly wrong is that Michal died, never having children, because David never touched her again. Some teach that this was God's punishment for her despising David as he danced before the Lord when the Ark of the Covenant was returned to Israel.

2 Samuel 6:23 (KJV)
Therefore Michal the daughter of Saul had no child unto the day
of her death.

The true story is that Michal died in childbirth. According to Jewish tradition, she cried out like a heifer while giving birth, and therefore her name was called "Eglah," which translates to heifer (female cow). This story is found in Genesis Rabbah 82:7 (also known as Bereshit Rabbah 82:7). The name Eglah appears in 2 Samuel 3:5, where she is listed as the mother of David's sixth son, Ithream:

2 Samuel 3:5 (KJV)
And the sixth, Ithream, by Eglah [heifer] David's wife.
These were born to David in Hebron.

An excellent article that explores this story further is "Michal, daughter of Saul: Midrash and Aggadah" by Tamar Kadari, available at jwa.org.

DOES "PUT AWAY" MEAN DIVORCE?

Many argue that the term "put away" means divorce.

> Matthew 19:9 (KJV)
> And I say unto you, Whosoever shall put away his wife, except [it be] for fornication, and shall marry another, committeth adultery: and whoso marrieth her which is put away doth commit adultery.

The Greek word for "put away" is apolyō, which means to set free, release, dismiss, or let go. It is derived from two Greek roots: apo, meaning "separation," and lyō, meaning "to loose" or "unbind."

According to the law of Moses, a man was first required to give his wife a bill of divorcement (get) before sending her out of his house. Simply "putting away" a wife without giving her a legal divorce was not considered a valid divorce under Jewish law.

> Deuteronomy 24:1 (KJV)
> When a man hath taken a wife, and married her, and it come to pass that she find no favour in his eyes, because he hath found some uncleanness in her: then *let him write her a bill of divorcement*, and give [it] in her hand, and *send her out of his house*.

The exact same process was required for a woman on her second marriage if divorced by her husband (Deuteronomy 24:3).

Deuteronomy 24:3 (KJV)
And [if] the latter husband hate her, and *write her a bill of divorcement*, and giveth [it] in her hand, and *sendeth her out of his house*; or if the latter husband die, which took her [to be] his wife;

According to the law of Moses, the proper order for divorce was as follows: first, give the woman her *get* (bill of divorcement), and then send her away. Simply sending a woman away without a formal bill of divorce was not considered a legal dissolution of the marriage.

Cohabitation was a major issue in ancient Israel. The law required the husband to provide food, clothing, and cohabitation for his wife, as seen in Exodus 21:10: "If he take him another wife; her food, her raiment, and her duty of marriage, shall he not diminish."

An entry titled "Husband and Wife" by Julius H. Greenstone on JewishEncyclopedia.com explains that a husband could not send his wife "away from his table" against her will, even if he provided her with sufficient financial support. In other words, a husband could not throw his wife out of the house. A wife, however, was permitted to leave the home under certain conditions—such as if her husband lived in a disreputable neighborhood or if he maltreated her. In such cases, he was still obligated to support her, no matter where she chose to reside.

If the husband was absent for a period, the court permitted the wife to draw financial support from his property. Even if she sold his property for her support without prior authorization, the sale remained valid. If she borrowed money to meet her needs during his absence, he was required to repay the debt upon his return. However, if someone gave her money voluntarily, they did so at their own risk and could not reclaim it from the husband—described metaphorically as "putting money on the horns of a deer." These rulings also applied in cases where the husband became mentally incapacitated (Yad, 12:10–22; Eben ha-'Ezer, 70).

According to JewishVirtualLibrary.org, a husband who refused to cohabit with his wife without just cause was labeled a ***mored***, meaning "rebellious husband." This designation was determined by priests. However, if the husband continued to meet his other obligations—such as providing food and clothing—he would not be given this status. If he persistently refused cohabitation, the woman had the right to request that her ***ketubah*** (marriage contract) be increased weekly, a sum she would receive once the divorce was granted. A wife whose husband was officially deemed a ***mored*** could demand a divorce, and the court had the authority to compel the husband to grant it.

On the other hand, if a wife refused cohabitation for longer than twelve months, the man was legally entitled to divorce her. In such a case, the wife would lose her ***ketubah*** and be designated a ***moredet*** (rebellious wife), as stated in Ketubot 63b.

In his 1884 book, The Jewish Law of Marriage and Divorce: In Ancient and Modern Times (pp. 124–125), Dr. Moses Mielziner outlined four specific circumstances in which the courts enforced divorce—even against the will of one or both parties:

1. When a contracted marriage was later deemed invalid. This included adulterous, incestuous, or unlawful remarriages, such as marrying a previously divorced wife who had since married another man.

2. In cases of willful adultery or suspicion of adultery by the wife, divorce was mandatory.

3. When a marriage produced no children within ten years, although this law was later modified.

4. When cohabitation was no longer viable due to serious health concerns, such as if one spouse contracted an incurable disease like leprosy. Divorce was not required if the other party consented to continue the marriage without physical intimacy.

Understanding these laws and cultural norms around cohabitation and divorce is essential. It's clear that cohabitation presented significant challenges in many marriages throughout ancient Israel. The complexities of cohabitation created loopholes in the legal system—loopholes that were often exploited and eventually addressed in religious teachings and legal reforms by the Sanhedrin. These cultural norms were the foundation of Jesus' teachings when He spoke against simply "putting away" a spouse without proper divorce procedures.

Women Could Not Initiate a Divorce

In ancient Israel, a woman could not initiate a divorce. This is a fact often acknowledged in Jewish tradition, yet it's rarely discussed within Christian teachings. Interestingly, despite this cultural and legal reality, very few seem to question Jesus' statement on the matter—particularly in light of the fact that His audience would have understood that only a man had the legal authority to issue a divorce.

Mark 10:12 (KJV)
And if a woman shall put away her husband, and be married to another, she committeth adultery.

Most bible translations state, "If a woman divorces her husband..."

Mark 10:12 (NKJV)
"And if a woman divorces her husband and marries another, she commits adultery."

A man had the right to divorce a woman for any cause and without her consent during that time. While many believe Jesus was restricting what constituted "just cause" for divorce, few realize that a woman could not initiate a divorce through the court. So, "put away" did not and could not mean divorce in Mark 10:12.

In fact, it was only about 1,000 years ago that Rebbeinu Gershom ben Yehuda (965–1028) issued a decree forbidding a husband from divorcing his wife without her consent. This ruling was accepted as binding by European Jewry.

In most cases, if a woman asked her husband for a divorce, he would grant it. However, if the husband refused, the woman could not initiate divorce proceedings directly through the court. Instead, she could petition the court to intervene, in which case she would be required to prove just cause. Therefore, the claim often made in Christian teachings—that women had no legal recourse in marriage—is inaccurate. And the claim that the woman could divorce but could not remarry is also false. Both claims are historically inaccurate. If a woman "put away" her husband, then she was only separated from him, but still legally married.

According to the Jewish Virtual Library article "Issues in Jewish Ethics: Divorce," a Jewish religious court could compel the husband to grant a divorce when there was just cause, such as when a husband refused marital relations, failed to support his wife, committed adultery, was abusive, or suffered from a loathsome disease such as leprosy.

Abuse was broadly defined and could include physical violence, cursing, ridicule, verbal insults (including toward in-laws), forbidding visits to in-laws, uncontrolled temper, or disrespectful language. A woman was not expected to live in such an environment.

Shottenstein commentary, explains the grounds upon which a husband can be "forced" (by the court) to divorce his wife. The Mishnah Ketubbot 7:10 (BT, Ketubbot 77a) "And these are the defects for which the court forces him to divorce her: One afflicted with boils; or one who has a polyp; or one who works as a gatherer, or one who works as a melder of copper, or one who works as a tanner of hides, all of whose work involves handling foul-smelling materials. Whether he had these defects before they got married, or whether they developed after they got married, the court forces them to divorce."

The Talmud in Yevamot (Yevamot 65b) explains that if the husband is found to be sterile, the court can compel the man to divorce his wife. The argument is that "a woman must be given the opportunity to bear a child in order to have someone to care for her in her old age."

Rebellious Husbands and Wives (*Mored* and *Moredet*)

Before we can examine what rebellious husbands and wives are, we must understand the woman was given the option to be independent or dependent. This choice determined how marital disputes were resolved by the court.

Dependent Wife vs Independent Wife

The woman had the option to choose if she wanted to be a dependent wife (isha teluya) and an independent wife (isha she'eina teluya). The Talmud (Ketubot 58b, 64b, 65b) discusses how the financial arrangements differed.

Dependent Wife (*Isha Teluya*)

A dependent wife relies on her husband for her basic sustenance—food, clothing, and shelter—as obligated by the ketubah (marriage contract) and Torah law (Exodus 21:10). According to rabbinic law, the earnings of a dependent wife (ma'aseh yadeha, "the work of her hands") belong to the husband. In exchange, the husband is fully obligated to provide for her needs. This arrangement was designed to ensure mutual benefit: the husband provides for his wife's sustenance, and her earnings help support the household. If her earnings exceed what is necessary for her maintenance, the excess may be retained by the husband unless a different agreement is made.

The Independent Wife (*Isha She'eina Teluya*)

A woman had the right to waive her husband's obligation to provide her with sustenance. This typically occurred when a wife had her own means of financial support, such as property, family wealth, or a business. In such cases, since she did not rely on her husband for daily maintenance, she retained full control over her own earnings (ma'aseh yadeha, "the work of her hands"). By choosing financial independence, she forfeited her right to demand full sustenance (mezonot—food, clothing, and shelter) and the level of conjugal support expected of a dependent wife. However, she did not forfeit her marital rights entirely. The husband remained obligated to fulfill her conjugal rights (onah), although the frequency of that obligation could adjust according to their circumstances.

Marital disputes were brought before the Beit Din (rabbinical court) and judged by a tribunal of three or more judges (dayanim). A woman's ketubah (marriage contract) would specify whether she was a dependent wife or an independent wife. If a dispute arose concerning financial support, a woman who had waived her right to sustenance could not later demand daily maintenance from her husband, as her choice of independence was legally binding.

A Rebellious Husband

What constitutes a rebellious husband (mored) or a rebellious wife (moredet)? This was not based on a spouse's personal feelings regarding their spouse. The law outlined a mored or a moredet. The court would declare the man or woman to be mored or moredet. Search "husband and wife" on jewishvirtuallibrary.org , as this is a subject too large to cover in its entirety.

A rebellious husband was one that refused to keep the "ten obligations toward his wife (or her descendants) and four rights in respect of her."

Proof that a husband was mored entitled the wife to demand "that he be obliged to grant her a divorce, and if necessary, that he be compelled to do so."

Ten Obligations (A Rebellious Husband):

1. Provide sustenance or maintenance.
2. Supply lodging and clothing.
3. Cohabit with her.
4. Provide the ketubah ("prenup"). If the ketubah was destroyed, it was required to be replaced. In such a case, a second ketubah is made up (called a Ketubah De'irkesa), which states in its opening phrase that it comes to substitute a previous ketubah that has been lost. Spouses were prohibited from living together if the ketubah had been destroyed, lost, or was otherwise unretrievable.
5. Procure medical attention and care in case of illness.
6. Ransom her if taken captive.
7. Provide suitable burial.
8. Provide support after his death (life insurance). Right to live in his house as long as she remained a widow.
9. Provide for the support of the daughters of the marriage from his estate after his death, until they become betrothed or reached the age of maturity.
10. Provide that the sons of the marriage shall inherit their mother's ketubbah, in addition to their rightful portion of the estate of their father, shared with his sons by other wives.

The husband's rights:

1. to the benefit of his wife's handiwork (the wife's earnings)
2. to her chance gains or finds
3. to the usufruct of her property
4. to inherit her estate

A Rebellious Wife

A rebellious wife (with no justification) fell under two categories:

a) an angry, quarrelsome wife who refuses to cohabit
b) refusing sexual relations.

This did not apply if the woman refused to cohabit with her husband but still fulfilled all of her other marital duties. If the woman's reason was genuine for refusing conjugal, the court would impel her to seek a divorce. In both cases, the woman lost her right to maintenance, and the husband would lose the right to woman's "handiwork" unless she were financially independent.

Failure to provide "legal justification" would result in the court impelling her to seek a divorce. In the case, for example, of her refusal to have sexual relations, she would lose her maintenance and, once divorced, would not receive her ketubah. Understand this depended "on conditions that differ according to the category of moredet." In the case of the woman refusing to cohabit with her husband, refusal must be no less than twelve months, at which point the husband was entitled to divorce the woman and she would forfeit her ketubah.

There were actions that were to be taken before the divorce. Under Jewish law (Halacha), if a marital dispute arises that cannot be resolved privately, either the husband or wife has the right—and in some cases, the obligation—to bring the matter before a Beit Din (rabbinical court) for intervention.

Grounds for Divorce

The following information is a summary from the article on Chabad. org entitled The Wife's Grounds for Divorce by Rabbi Reuven P. Bulka.

"Much as divorce is not a desideratum within Jewish life, neither is the locking in of either husband or wife in a prison of misery." Rabbi Bulka explains that the law warned against taking advantage of orphans and widows. The idea that the law would leave women vulnerable within the marriage is unrealistic. The Torah forbids the affliction of others; why would it be allowed or tolerated at the hands of a husband?

The Wife's Grounds for Divorce:

I will briefly list the reasons divorce was permitted. If the husband neglects or abuses the basic marital needs. The neglect of sustenance or conjugal visitation violated a primary responsibility of the marital covenant. It was not permitted to be used by "the husband as a weapon with which to deprive the wife, either emotionally or physically, is considered a breach of the sacred marital trust."

A husband philandering with other women. (Proof of adultery was not necessary; however, men could not be charged with adultery unless the other woman was married.) The husband philandering with other women caused her a bad name. This was "just cause."

If the wife feels repulsed by her husband. This may have been caused by a repulsive blemish, "a noxious habit," or an intolerable stench possibly due to his line of work. Certain trades, like tanning, produced an odor that a lot of women found unbearable. This was applicable even if the woman was aware of the man's vocation and had the best intentions, but later found it intolerable.

Shottenstein commentary, explains the grounds upon which a husband can be "forced" by the court to divorce his wife. Though women could not initiate a divorce, the court would intervene for just cause, impelling the man to initiate the divorce. Below are circumstances in which the court viewed as just cause.

The Mishnah Ketubbot 7:10 (BT, Ketubbot 77a) "And these are the defects for which the court forces him to divorce her: One afflicted with boils; or one who has a polyp; or one who works as a gatherer, or one who works as a melder of copper, or one who works as a tanner of hides, all of whose work involves handling foul-smelling materials. Whether he had these defects before they got married, or whether they developed after they got married, the court forces them to divorce." The Talmud in Yevamot (Yevamot 65b) explains that if the husband is found to be sterile, the court can compel the man to divorce his wife. The argument is that "a woman must be given the opportunity to bear a child in order to have someone to care for her in her old age."

If the woman made a vow that affects the marital union and the husband fails to annul the vow, this was viewed as the husband's desire to sever the relationship (Numbers 30:8). If the husband vowed a vow not allowing the wife to work, this was sufficient grounds for divorce. The reasoning was that idleness potentially leads to frustration and worse, so "no wife can be coerced into such an adversity."

Abuse included hitting, cursing, ridiculing, insults, insulting in-laws, or forbidding visits to in-laws, temperamental outbursts, or disrespectful language. The wife was not expected to live in such an environment. The woman's claim to the court had to prove that this was the husband's normal demeanor. If the husband counterclaimed that his behavior was a result of the wife, the burden of proof fell on his shoulders.

If the husband moved his mother into the home and it "restricted the wife's freedom." If the husband forced the wife to have conjugal relations during her menstrual period may also demand a divorce. These two arguments were based on the woman was entitled to freedom, dignity, and respect beyond any question.

"The wife is likewise not considered a moredet if she leaves the house because the husband has failed to live up to his maintenance responsibilities. In fact, in such an instance, the husband is considered to be the instigator." She's also not labeled a moredet for leaving due to issues created by her in-laws.

The husband who is a mored must give his wife a divorce, and must also give her the marriage settlement known as the ketubah. The wife who is a moredet may be divorced by her husband, and she forfeits her right to the ketubah settlement.

Steps Taken Before Divorce

The wife could not declare her husband a rebellious husband, and the husband could not declare his wife a rebellious wife. The court (judges) would have to declare a husband to be mored and a wife to be moredet. Before reaching this decision steps of intervention would be taken by the court. The Mishnah explains (Ket. 63a) that a rebellious wife's ketubah would be diminished from week to week until nothing remained. The husband could then divorce her without owing the woman her ketubah, so the woman lost her divorce settlement. Other procedures were adopted such as warnings issued by the court. Public announcements were also made in the synagogue for several weeks. She would be informed that upon final warning she was in danger of losing her ketubah and being labeled moredet.

The wife did not forfeit her dowry even when she had forfeited her ketubah. The dowry is regarded as her own property. Under Jewish law, land deeds that were either owned by the woman prior to marriage (Nichsei Milog) or given to her as part of her dowry (Nichsei Tzon Barzel) remained legally in her name, even though the husband had the right to collect the usufruct (fruits, profits, or benefits) from the property during the marriage.

In regard to the rebellious husband, he is also warned by the court. The Mishnah explains (Ket. 63a) if he continues to transgress the command Exodus 21:10 the ketubah would be increased. However, the man did have the option to divorce his wife immediately and pay her her ketubah, and thus has not transgressed the law because he "never withheld."

The Wife's Grounds for Divorce by Rabbi Reuven P. Bulka explains what happens when a man refuses to divorce his wife while also refusing to cohabit. "Refusal to cohabit with his wife, she is entitled to demand that the amount of her ketubbah be increased from week to week, as may be determined by the court, and to receive the increased ketubbah upon the grant of the divorce."

We can see this warning made to the priest by the prophet Malachi in Malachi 2:16.

Malachi 2:16 (KJV)
For the LORD, the God of Israel, saith that he hateth putting away: for [one] covereth violence with his garment, saith the LORD of hosts: therefore take heed to your spirit, that ye ***deal not treacherously***.

Malachi 2:16 (RSV) For I hate divorce, says the LORD the God of Israel, and covering one's garment with violence, says the LORD of hosts. So take heed to yourselves and ***do not be faithless***.

This passage is the scripture many use to argue that God hates divorce. The Hebrew word for divorce is not used in the verse. The word used is šālaḥ, which means putting away or sending away. This was the refusal to cohabit. The Hebrew word for divorce is kᵊrîṯûṯ. This passage does not say, "God hates divorce." The King James Version has the accurate translation, "he hateth putting away." If the priest that Malachi were sent to did not listen and change, they would be considered mored (rebellious husbands) by the court. This was a public warning issued to them by the prophet.

In Malachi 2:15, the prophet Malachi rebukes the priests, emphasizing that God desires "godly seed"—offspring raised in covenant faithfulness. Yet, these priests had failed in their conjugal obligations to their wives, violating the terms of their ketubah (marriage contract). According to Exodus 21:10, a husband is required to provide his wife with food, clothing, and marital intimacy. By neglecting these duties, the priests not only transgressed the Torah but broke faith with their wives, dissolving the sanctity of their marriage covenant.

Malachi 2:14 (NLT)
You cry out, "Why doesn't the LORD accept my worship?" I'll tell you why! Because the LORD witnessed the vows you and your wife made when you were young. But *you have been unfaithful* [treacherous] to her, though she remained your faithful partner, the wife of your marriage vows.

So, Was Jesus Being Prophetic?

Was Jesus' statement in Mark 10:12 referring to a future time when women would be permitted to divorce their husbands?

No. Jesus was speaking about women who had left their husbands— women who had "put away" their spouses, but were still legally married. These women were forbidden to remarry until they received a get (a bill of divorce). To enter another marriage without a get rendered the new union adulterous in the eyes of the law.

Women did have the right to leave their husbands. Refusal to cohabitate was common in Israel. Therefore, Jesus' statement about a woman being "put away" (apolyō) but not legally divorced makes sense in context. A woman who is separated (apolyō) and marries another man is committing adultery because she is still legally married.

It's important to note that Jesus never made this statement publicly. He never addressed it to the scribes, Sadducees, or Pharisees, who were experts in the law. Instead, He spoke these words privately to His disciples, behind closed doors.

Mark 10:10 (KJV)
And in the house his disciples asked him again of the same [matter].

Such an argument would have made little sense to present publicly, since it was already unlawful for a separated woman to remarry. A priest would never marry a divorced woman who did not have her bill of divorcement. This was not only prohibited in Israel but also in most societies where polyandry was outlawed. Under U.S. law, for instance, state laws against bigamy require that a previous marriage be annulled before a new one can be recognized. In Israel, a woman would have to obtain a divorce from both husbands if she had entered into a second marriage. So why would Jesus even need to make such a statement?

At the time, a very public and scandalous divorce had recently taken place in Israel, where a woman had divorced her husband without the court's approval. The Jewish courts did not consider this a lawful divorce. This incident prompted John the Baptist to make public statements against the situation. John—Jesus' cousin—was eventually imprisoned and beheaded at the request of the woman involved (Matthew 14).

The Jewish historian Josephus also documented this controversial divorce. In Antiquities 18.5.4, Josephus wrote, "Herodias took upon her to confound the laws of our country, and divorced herself from her husband while he was alive, and was married to Herod [Antipas], her husband's brother by the father's side, he was tetrarch of Galilee." This woman, Herodias, is also mentioned in Matthew 14.

Josephus also recorded another case of a woman initiating divorce. Salome, the sister of Herod the Great (who sought to kill Jesus as a baby—Matthew 2), was first married to her uncle Joseph (Antiquities 15:65). After accusing him of seducing Herod's wife, Joseph was executed. Salome then married an Idumean aristocrat, Costobarus, whom she later divorced. Costobarus was also eventually killed by Herod (Antiquities 15:253–266).

In Antiquities 15.7.10, Josephus explains: "She [Salome] sent him [Costobarus] a bill of divorce and dissolved her marriage with him, though this was not according to the Jewish law. For with us, it is lawful for a husband to do so; but a wife, if she departs from her husband, cannot of herself be married to another, unless her former husband put her away. However, Salome chose to follow not the law of her country, but the law of her authority, and so renounced her wedlock."

The statements made by Jesus and those recorded by Josephus align: it was unlawful for a woman to dissolve the marriage on her own. The man was required to "put away" the woman, and the woman needed to receive a get (a bill of divorce). However, several problematic trends had become normal in Israel. These loopholes in the law were being exploited.

ISRAEL'S THREE COURT LEVELS

Most Christians are unfamiliar with the Jewish court system or the legal process Moses established. In Israel, the lowest court level was responsible for handling civil matters like divorce. The Jewish court of law is called the Beit Din. The court system was made up of three levels:

The Great Sanhedrin (The High Court)

The high court was known as the Beit Din HaGadol, meaning "Great House of Law." It was equivalent to the U.S. Supreme Court and was comprised of 71 elders. This court was first established by Moses in Numbers 11, where 70 elders were appointed to assist him. Joshua took Moses' place as judge following his death. In the book of Judges, individuals like Gideon, Deborah, Samson, and later Eli and Samuel, served in Moses' seat.

Some have argued that Deborah was only chosen by God as a replacement. However, she was not a substitute as prophet or judge over the nation. The idea of a "replacement" comes from the incident where Barak refused to go to war without Deborah, and as a result, Jael (who drove a tent peg into the enemy general's temple) received the glory that would have gone to Barak. Songs were even written in Jael's honor (Judges 5:24). Jael replaced Barak in receiving glory for the victory, as Deborah prophesied in Joshua 4:9.

Deborah, on the other hand, sat in the seat of Moses along with the other 70 elders, as required for the Great Sanhedrin. When reading the book of Judges and considering the judges (Othniel, Gideon, Deborah, Samson, Eli, and Samuel), we must picture them judging Israel alongside 70 elders. All those selected by God to be judges "sat in the seat of Moses" (Matthew 23:2).

This court convened in Jerusalem on the Temple Mount. According to Britannica.com (search: "Great Sanhedrin"), the court's responsibilities included "appointing the king and the high priest, declaring war, and expanding the territory of Jerusalem and the Temple. Judicially, it could try a high priest, a false prophet, a rebellious elder, or an errant tribe."

The Lesser Sanhedrin (The Lower Court)

This court was typically found in larger cities in Israel—specifically in cities with more than 120 men. Each case was presided over by 23 judges. The Lesser Sanhedrin handled capital crimes.

There were thirty-six offenses that warranted the death penalty, including murder, adultery, idolatry, and desecration of the Sabbath. Even civil cases, such as slander, could be heard here if they implied adultery—since adultery was a capital offense.

The Beit Din (The Tribunal Court)

This court was usually presided over by three judges, though sometimes five or seven were appointed. At least one of the three judges had to be a rabbi, while the others were required to be knowledgeable in the law.

The Beit Din dealt with minor civil matters, including divorce (property division, custody, and visitation), ḥaliẓah (release from levirate marriage), conversion to Judaism, the absolution of vows, and cases involving theft when the thief could not repay the victim. Common cases included marriage, matrimonial disputes, family and rabbinic contract disputes, inheritance, commercial law, real estate, and financial matters, congregational issues, employer-employee, landlord-tenant, breach of contract, and more. Punishments in this court typically involved flogging (forty lashes minus one) or a fine.

For more detailed information, visit JewishVirtualLibrary.com and search for "Israel Judicial Branch: Beit Din & Judges From Bible to Modern Times."

Jesus referenced this court system in His Sermon on the Mount. The "judgment" referred to the Tribunal Courts (the Beit Din), and the "council" referred to the Sanhedrin.

Matthew 5:22 (KJV)
But I say unto you, That whosoever is angry with his brother without a cause shall be in danger of *the judgment*: and whosoever shall say to his brother, Raca, shall be in danger of *the council*: but whosoever shall say, Thou fool, shall be in danger of hell fire.

The Accused

Moses required that no person could be put to death without facing their accusers.

Deuteronomy 19:17 (KJV) Then **both** the men, between whom the controversy is, **shall stand before the Lord, before the priests and the judges**, which shall be in those days;

Two or Three Witnesses

Hebrews 10:28 (KJV)
He that despised Moses' law died without mercy under two or three witnesses:

Those who refused to obey the law were subject to fines, flogging, or even death—depending on the type of crime committed. The statement in

Hebrews 10:28 has led many Christians to claim that the law was merciless. However, it's important to understand that mercy presumes guilt. In other words, mercy is shown to someone who is indeed guilty. The courts in Israel, however, took extensive measures to ensure a person was truly guilty before passing judgment.

For instance, a single witness was never enough to convict someone, even in capital crimes such as murder (Numbers 35:30). The law required the testimony of two or three eyewitnesses to convict someone (Deuteronomy 17:6; Deuteronomy 19:15).

This raises an important question: Who could and could not serve as a witness?

Who Could and Could Not Serve as a Witness?

The Universal Jewish Encyclopedia in 10 Volumes: An Authoritative and Popular Presentation of Jews and Judaism Since the Earliest Times, Volume 1, under the entry for "Acquittal," explains who was disqualified from giving testimony in both civil and criminal cases. Disqualified individuals included: women, slaves, minors, relatives, friends or enemies of the accused, and those disqualified due to minor offenses or bad habits. Additionally, any relatives of the defendant or the judges were barred from testifying.

Relatives could not serve as valid witnesses together in a legal case. Mishnan, Sanhedrin 3:4, explicitly states that relatives are disqualified as witnesses. For example, a father and son, or brothers, could not testify in the same case. Babylonian Talmud, Sanhedrin 27b expands on this, explaining that relatives up to a certain degree (including by marriage) were excluded, because of the likelihood of bias. Maimonides, Mishneh Torah (Laws of Testimony, 13:1-3) codifies the same rule, explaining that no testimony from close relatives, whether in capital cases or financial disputes, is permitted. Under US law, there are certain "testimonial privileges" that allow people to refuse to testify or keep certain communications confidential, such as Spousal Privilege, Attorney-Client Privilege, Doctor-Patient Privilege, and Psychotherapist-Patient Privilege.

Women were not always excluded from being witnesses. There were occasions when women were permitted—or even required—to serve as witnesses, especially if a crime occurred in locations where men did not frequent. For further study, see Rabbi Aaron Mackler's paper titled "Edut Nashim K'Edut Anashim: The Testimony of Women is as the Testimony of Men: A Concurring Opinion."

Diligent Inquiries (Thorough Investigations)

All judges were required to make diligent inquiries into each case. This was especially crucial in capital punishment cases, where a person's life was at stake. Judges were not allowed to make assumptions or render verdicts lightly.

According to the Jewish Encyclopedia (search term: "Acquittal in Talmudic Law"), the court proceedings placed a strong emphasis on justice and caution. It notes:

"It was deemed the highest duty of the judges to see that no innocent man be condemned; in fact, that no one should be convicted who was not guilty both morally and legally, and whose guilt was not established in a strictly legal way. For this purpose, they were to carry on a most searching cross-examination of the prosecuting witnesses."

We see this requirement clearly stated in Deuteronomy 19:18, where judges are instructed to conduct a thorough investigation into the claims brought before them.

Deuteronomy 19:18 (KJV)
And the judges shall make *diligent inquisition*: and, behold, [if] the witness [be] a false witness, [and] hath testified falsely against his brother;

Deuteronomy 19:18 (NIV)
The judges must make a ***thorough investigation***, and if the
witness proves to be a liar, giving false testimony against a fellow
Israelite,

The witnesses were required to be separated and interrogated individually by all twenty-three judges. Any discrepancies in their testimonies would result in an acquittal. Additionally, the witnesses had to be either eye or ear witnesses—they needed to have personal knowledge of the event or fact in question. Hearsay was not permitted.

The Universal Jewish Encyclopedia in 10 Volumes: An Authoritative and Popular Presentation of Jews and Judaism Since the Earliest Times, Volume 1, under the entry for "Acquittal," explains that witnesses were required to warn the accused of the serious nature of the act they were about to commit and the specific penalty they would face. The warning had to be so clear and direct that the accused must have replied that they still intended to go through with the act, despite understanding the consequences.

Leviticus 19:17 (KJV) Thou shalt not hate thy brother in thine heart: thou shalt in any wise rebuke thy neighbour, and not suffer sin upon him.

It was a Jewish person's obligation to prevent their neighbor from sinning—which, to a Jew, meant stopping them from committing a crime. During court proceedings, the judges would ask the witness what actions they took to try to prevent the individual from committing the offense. If the witness failed to intervene, it could result in an acquittal.

"Thou Shalt Not Bear False Witness"

Exodus 20:16 (KJV)
Thou shalt not bear false witness against thy neighbour.

It is surprising how many Christians interpret this commandment in the Ten Commandments as simply meaning "don't lie" or "don't spread lies about your neighbor." However, this law was a legal statute enforced in court and carried serious consequences—even the death penalty. If it was determined that the witnesses were lying, they were to suffer the same punishment intended for the accused. In capital cases, false witnesses and conspirators were put to death.

Deuteronomy 19:18-20 (KJV)

18. And the judges shall make diligent inquisition: and, behold, [if] the witness [be] a false witness, [and] hath testified falsely against his brother;

19. ***Then shall ye do unto him, as he had thought to have done unto his brother***: so shalt thou put the evil away from among you.

20. And those which remain shall hear, and fear, and shall henceforth commit no more any such evil among you.

Exodus 23:1-3 (Amplified)

1. You shall not give a false report; you shall not join hands with the wicked to be a malicious witness [promoting wrong and violence].

2. You shall not follow a crowd to do [something] evil, nor shall you testify at a trial or in a dispute so as to side with a crowd in order to pervert justice;

3. nor shall you favor or be partial to a poor man in his dispute [simply because he is poor].

Trials and Acquittals

The Universal Jewish Encyclopedia in 10 Volumes: An Authoritative and Popular Presentation of Jews and Judaism Since the Earliest Times, Volume 1, explains how verdicts were determined:

"Verdicts were determined by majority vote, but even then, there was a difference in favor of the accused. While a majority of one was sufficient to acquit, a majority of two was necessary for conviction. If the first vote resulted in a majority of one for conviction, two new judges were added to the original Sanhedrin of twenty-three, and a new vote was taken. If the majority of one still persisted, judges were added pair by pair until the total reached seventy-one. Then, if the vote was still one in favor of conviction, an acquittal was decreed."

The Talmud (Sanhedrin 17a) explains that if the Sanhedrin unanimously voted for conviction, the accused had to be freed. The Talmud (Sanhedrin 3b) clarifies this principle, stating that in every trial, some point in favor of the accused must be advanced; otherwise, the trial is incomplete. The Universal Jewish Encyclopedia in 10 Volumes further explains the concept of "acquittal," stating, "After a verdict of conviction had been given, it could be changed. The final decision of the court was delayed for a day, in the hope that some new evidence in favor of the accused might be brought to light." The case could be reopened for the defense by the accused themselves, allowing them a final word of self-defense—even on their way to execution.

A "no" vote was not permitted; the judge would be required to excuse themselves. Judges were also permitted to change their vote from conviction to acquittal. However, if a vote of acquittal had been made, they could no longer vote for conviction. Cases that ended in acquittals could not be retried.

Guilty Verdicts

If the accused was found guilty, the witnesses were required to be the first to place their hands on the convicted.

Deuteronomy 17:6-7 (KJV)
6. At the mouth of two witnesses, or three witnesses, shall he that is worthy of death be put to death; but at the mouth of one witness he shall not be put to death.
7. The hands of the witnesses shall be first upon him to put him to death, and afterward the hands of all the people. So thou shalt put the evil away from among you.

This law requires witnesses who testify to understand the gravity of their testimony. If their testimony could result in a person losing their life, they were required to be the first participants in the act. They had to "cast the first stone." Then, the entire congregation was to participate. However, this was not a standard rule, as some crimes were to be executed by the hands of the priest.

In Leviticus 24, we have an account of an Israelite boy who blasphemed the name of God. This was a capital offense punishable by death. Verses 13-16 explain how his sentence was executed.

Leviticus 24:13-16 (ESV)

13. Then the LORD spoke to Moses, saying,

14. "Bring out of the camp the one who cursed, and let all who heard him lay their hands on his head, and let all the congregation stone him.

15. And speak to the people of Israel, saying, Whoever curses his God shall bear his sin.

16. Whoever blasphemes the name of the LORD shall surely be put to death. All the congregation shall stone him. The sojourner as well as the native, when he blasphemes the Name, shall be put to death.

The Sanhedrin Rather Acquits

Many teach that the Sanhedrin was a murderous court, and some view the law as merciless, with Jesus' teachings of love and grace being seen as contradictory to the law. However, this is far from accurate. Israel's legal system took every possible measure not to find a guilty verdict. The mindset of the court was described by the Jewish legal theorist Moses Maimonides, who wrote in the 1100s, "It is better and more satisfactory to acquit a thousand guilty persons than to put a single innocent one to death."

Rabbi Elazar ben Azarya stated that "a Sanhedrin which condemned one man to death in seventy years would be called a 'murderous Sanhedrin.'" Yet, such was the spirit of the Jewish law, which believed that one who unjustly destroys a single soul is as if they had destroyed an entire world. The law went to great lengths to prevent such a misfortune. This quote from the Talmud (Sanhedrin 37a) illustrates the carefulness with which the Sanhedrin approached the taking of a life. It compares the act of taking the life of a Jew to destroying an entire world, much like the responsibility Adam bore through his actions.

Here is the quote from Sanhedrin 37a:

Sanhedrin 37a: "The court tells the witnesses: Therefore, Adam, the first man, was created alone, to teach you that with regard to anyone who destroys one soul from the Jewish people—i.e., kills one Jew—the verse ascribes him blame as if he destroyed an entire world, as Adam was one person, from whom the population of an entire world came forth. And conversely, anyone who sustains (saves) one soul from the Jewish people, the verse ascribes him credit as if he sustained (saves) an entire world."

The Sanhedrin did everything in its power to render a just verdict. In keeping with the law of Moses, the Sanhedrin preferred to release a guilty person rather than to kill an innocent one. God required the court to judge in this way, and He promised to take care of any guilty person released by the court.

Exodus 23:7 (NIV)
Have nothing to do with a false charge and do not put an innocent
or honest person to death, for I will not acquit the guilty.

The Woman Caught in Adultery

In the book of John, the scribes and Pharisees brought a woman to Jesus who had been caught in the act of adultery. They told Him that the Law of Moses required her to be stoned to death, but they asked what He had to say. Their intent was to trap Jesus into saying something contrary to the law. Instead of responding immediately, Jesus stooped down and began writing on the ground with His finger. Finally, He said, "He that is without sin among you, let him first cast a stone at her." Convicted by their own consciences, the men left one by one.

John 8:10-11 (KJV)
10. When Jesus had lifted up himself, and saw none but the woman, he said unto her, Woman, where are those thine accusers? hath no man condemned thee?
11. She said, No man, Lord. And Jesus said unto her, Neither do I condemn thee: go, and sin no more.

Some teach that Jesus did not condemn the woman for the sin of adultery because He did away with capital punishment altogether. This would imply that Jesus changed the entire law for the nation of Israel, which would be comparable to changing the U.S. Constitution. It would suggest that Jesus abolished all 36 capital crimes in Israel, including murder.

The commonly taught lesson from this story is that Jesus showed the woman mercy. On a Sunday morning, you might hear it explained that Jesus is always ready and willing to forgive and extend His grace. If we sin, we can look to Jesus, who will forgive us and cover our guilt.

While this may be true, if we examine this story through the lens of the law of Moses, we come to a different conclusion. Jesus said, "He that is without sin among you, let him first cast a stone at her." For Christians, the word "sin" refers to an act that goes against moral, ethical, or religious laws. If we commit such an act, we can ask God for forgiveness, and He is faithful and just to forgive us. However, for the Jewish people, the word "sin" also means "crime." In Jewish thought, sin refers to a legal offense, not just a moral failing.

So, Jesus was telling the men that the one who had not committed a "crime" could cast the first stone. Though it is often taught that His statement about casting the first stone is a New Testament concept, this is not true.

Deuteronomy 17:7 (KJV)
The hands of the witnesses shall be first upon him to put him to death, and afterward the hands of all the people. So thou shalt put the evil away from among you.

Deuteronomy 17:7 (NLT)
The witnesses must throw the first stones, and then all the people may join in. In this way, you will purge the evil from among you.

Once again, Jesus quoted the Law of Moses in response to the scribes and Pharisees. According to the law, the witnesses were required to throw the first stone; their hands had to be the first to put the guilty party to death. Additionally, a single witness was not enough to sentence someone to death; the law required the testimony of two or three witnesses.

Deuteronomy 17:5-6 (KJV)
5. Then shalt thou bring forth that man or that woman, which have committed that wicked thing, unto thy gates, [even] that man or that woman, and shalt stone them with stones, till they die.
6. At the mouth of two witnesses, or three witnesses, shall he that is worthy of death be put to death; [but] at the mouth of one witness he shall not be put to death.

The witnesses were required to be eyewitnesses; hearsay was not permissible. The requirement of two or three eyewitnesses also applied to capital crimes, such as murder.

Numbers 35:30 (KJV)
Whoso killeth any person, the murderer shall be put to death by the mouth of witnesses: but one witness shall not testify against any person [to cause him] to die.

The woman brought to Jesus was not given a trial, nor was she permitted to face her accusers.

Deuteronomy 19:16-18 (NLT)

16. "If a malicious witness comes forward and accuses someone of a crime,

17. then **both the accuser and accused must appear** before the LORD by coming to the priests and judges in office at that time.

18. The judges must investigate the case thoroughly. If the accuser has brought false charges against his fellow Israelite,

Since adultery was a capital crime, the law required her to stand before the lesser Sanhedrin, a court of 23 judges, to plead her case. The 23 judges were required to thoroughly investigate the crime. Under Jewish law, the judges were to make a "diligent inquisition" of the witnesses, not the accused. Those who brought the woman to Jesus would have been questioned individually to make sure there was no contradiction in their testimony.

Witnesses were not permitted to lie on the stand (forswear), nor could they follow the crowd in doing wrong. Twisting justice was strictly forbidden. In this case, a crowd brought the woman to Jesus, breaking Exodus 23:1-2, not knowing if the woman was guilty or not.

Exodus 23:1-2 (NLT)

1. "You must not pass along false rumors. You must not cooperate with evil people by lying on the witness stand.

2. "You must not follow the crowd in doing wrong. When you are called to testify in a dispute, do not be swayed by the crowd to twist justice.

Another law broken in this story was that the woman was not warned about the crime she was committing before being taken. Jewish law required a person to confront their neighbor if they have wronged you or are sinning. They had a duty to rebuke those in the wrong. The commandment of tokheha means "you shall surely rebuke."

Leviticus 19:17 (NLT)
Do not nurse hatred in your heart for any of your relatives.
Confront people directly so you will not be held guilty for their sin.

Leviticus 19:17 (BBE)
Let there be no hate in your heart for your brother; but you may make a protest to your neighbour, so that he may be stopped from doing evil.

In addition, the woman was accused of the crime of adultery, yet the man involved was not present. Under Jewish law, for a woman to be charged with adultery, she had to be married. This would also mean that the man who was with her was guilty of adultery as well. Leviticus 20:10 required both the man and the woman to be brought before the judges, and if found guilty, both were to be put to death. In this case, no man was being accused of being an adulterer.

Though many believe that Jesus wrote the personal sins of the men on the ground, He may have simply been writing the Law of Moses. These men had violated many laws and were, therefore, guilty themselves. "He who is without sin, let him cast the first stone."

Jesus then said to the woman, "Where are those who accuse you?" Since no witnesses were present to bring an accusation, she could not be found guilty of her crime. Though mercy, long-suffering, and grace are often attributed to Jesus, these are, in fact, the very characteristics of God.

Psalms 103:6-13 (NLT)

6. The LORD gives righteousness and justice to all who are treated unfairly.

7. He revealed his character to Moses and his deeds to the people of Israel.

8. The LORD is compassionate and merciful, slow to get angry and filled with unfailing love.

9. He will not constantly accuse us, nor remain angry forever.

10. He does not punish us for all our sins; he does not deal harshly with us, as we deserve.

11. For his unfailing love toward those who fear him is as great as the height of the heavens above the earth.

12. He has removed our sins as far from us as the east is from the west.

13. The LORD is like a father to his children, tender and compassionate to those who fear him.

Exodus 34:5-6 (NLT)

5. Then the LORD came down in a cloud and stood there with him; and he called out his own name, Yahweh.

6. The LORD passed in front of Moses, calling out, "Yahweh! The LORD! The God of compassion and mercy! I am slow to anger and filled with unfailing love and faithfulness.

God and His Law are Just

Romans 7:12 (KJV)
Wherefore the law [is] holy, and the commandment holy, and just, and good.

Paul explained that the law is holy, good, and just. "Just" means the law was fair. The courts were required to demand honesty. God required the court to take great care to avoid shedding innocent blood, starting with who could testify, the interrogation of witnesses, the obligation of witnesses to prevent the crime from occurring, the punishment of witnesses for false testimony, a unanimous "guilty" vote resulting in an automatic acquittal, and the judges' inability to change an innocent vote to guilty. The judges' entire focus wasn't on finding people guilty of breaking the law but on righteous judgment.

The American judicial system is referred to as the "justice system," yet guilty people are sometimes found innocent and innocent people are sometimes found guilty. Judges are not required to investigate and interrogate to uncover innocence but instead try cases based solely on the evidence presented. In the U.S. judicial system, many people plead guilty to lesser charges out of fear of being found guilty, even if they may be innocent. This is not a system designed to determine innocence or guilt. In Israel, however, the judges didn't have to worry about guilt, as the Lord said He would not "acquit the guilty." In my opinion, this is the most just system I have ever seen. This truth contradicts the many Christian preachers who have taught that the Sanhedrin and the law were merciless and bloodthirsty. It was the complete opposite. The God of the Old Testament is no different from the God of the New Testament; He never changed. So, why would we expect anything different from the God of mercy and grace?

WHAT IN THE WORLD WAS GOING ON IN ISRAEL

The *Agunah* Crisis

The first question we must ask is: Why was Jesus addressing women being separated (put away) from their husbands and entering into another marriage without first being legally divorced so often? He called it adultery, and the court system did as well. Was there a social problem Jesus was addressing? Yes, there were several.

The law forbade a rabbi from marrying a woman who did not present her get (bill of divorcement). This was done to avoid accidentally marrying a married woman, thus making her second marriage adulterous. A woman could not initiate a divorce, and if the husband was missing, the court could not compel him to divorce her. Because of this, the Jews had a Hebrew word, agunah, used to describe women whose husbands were unwilling or unable to grant them a divorce. Traditionally, this term referred to women whose husbands disappeared during wartime or at sea.

To avoid this complication during wartime, all Israelite soldiers were required to give their wives a "conditional get." However, over time, agunah became associated with women whose husbands refused to grant them a divorce and give them a get.

A Conditional Divorce (*Get Al T'nai*)

A conditional get, or bill of divorce, is a document that a husband can give to his wife, which only takes effect if he doesn't return within a specified time period. The Hebrew term for a conditional get is get al t'nai, sometimes referred to as a t'nai get. This practice was and is used to prevent a woman from becoming agunah, a "chained woman" who could never remarry again. In Israel, soldiers would give their wives a conditional divorce before heading into war to prevent the woman from becoming an agunah and unable to remarry in case the soldier died in battle without proof or became a prisoner of war. As explained in Mishnah Gittin 7:3, a conditional divorce allowed a woman to avoid the obligation of levirate marriage (yibbum) in cases where her husband died childless. The get al t'nai also spared her the public embarrassment of halitzah (chalitzah), the ceremony in which the brother-in-law formally refuses to marry her.

It was this loophole (get al t'nai) that King David exploited with Bathsheba. King David took Bathsheba and laid with her. When her husband Uriah the Hittite later died in battle per David's instructions, her conditional get (get al t'nai) became retroactive to the point when Uriah was still living, thus making Bathsheba a divorced woman when David took her.

Sefaria.org, in Ketubot 9b, explains the conditional bill of divorce and references the passage 1 Samuel 17:18.

1 Samuel 17:18 (KJV)
And carry these ten cheeses unto the captain of [their] thousand, and look how thy brethren fare, and ***take their pledge***.

The pledge David received from his brothers in 1 Samuel 17:18 was their conditional divorces. David took advantage of the law, so he and Bathsheba did not commit adultery by the letter of the law. Uriah disobeyed a direct order from the king and was guilty of treason, which was a capital offense. David had the right to have Uriah killed for disobeying a direct order, but instead, he had him placed at the front line of the battle where he died. So, once again, David committed "no crime." Many Christians teach that David got away with adultery and murder because he was the king. This is not true. David exploited the law. What David did was lawful by the letter of the law but extremely unethical and immoral.

This is why Nathan the prophet was sent to David. God judged David by his heart and not the letter of the law. David was guilty, and God punished him. God spared David's life (2 Samuel 12:3), which, if David had been guilty of adultery, would have warranted his death. Instead, God invoked the law of "an eye for an eye." God took a sheep for a sheep. David took Uriah's sheep, who was Bathsheba according to Nathan's analogy, and so God took David's baby. Many preach that because David was king, he was not prosecuted by the court, which is not true. Unlike other nations, the kings of Israel were not above the law (Deuteronomy 17:18). If prosecuted, David would not have been found guilty of adultery or murder because of the conditional divorce and Uriah's treason. However, David's family suffered for his decision, costing the lives of several of his children and the violation of his daughter Tamar. God told David the sword would never leave his house (2 Samuel 12:10).

Ketubot 9b explains the conditional divorce requirement for soldiers.

The *Agunah* Problem

Like David, many Israelite men exploited the law of Moses. When it was not wartime, by disappearing, they could avoid giving their wives a get.

Why wouldn't the men simply divorce their wives? Why would they choose to abandon their wives? It was because divorce was very expensive.

The law of Moses required a marriage agreement to begin the betrothal (engagement). The ketubah (the marriage agreement) stated that the man would pay the woman a divorce settlement. It was common for men to agree that this payment would be equal to the woman's dowry. In addition to the divorce settlement, the man had to return the woman's dowry to her. And the dowry might have been land, in which the man could receive usufruct.

Once the ketubah was signed, the couple required a divorce to end the marriage or betrothal (engagement). We can see this law and cultural norm in the story of Joseph and Mary.

Joseph and Mary

Joseph and Mary were betrothed when Mary became pregnant through the power of the Holy Spirit. Under Jewish law, once a couple is betrothed, the woman is legally bound to the man, but they may not consummate the marriage until the final ceremony (nissuin). If Mary had been with another man, Joseph would have been defiled by proceeding with the marriage. Scripture tells us that Joseph, being a just man, did not want to publicly shame Mary, so he wrestled with how to handle the situation. As a righteous man, Joseph was likely not considering abandoning her entirely—doing so would have made Mary an agunah, a "chained" woman unable to remarry. While a man didn't require a bill of divorcement to remarry, without formally divorcing his betrothed the woman remained bound to him, requiring a get. If Joseph had quietly left, people may have assumed he had gotten Mary pregnant before the nissuin. According to Jewish scholars Marcus Jastrow and Lewis N. Dembitz, such an act was not a capital offense but was still considered lewd. It wouldn't have been a crime, but Joseph would have been seen as weak and dishonorable.

Matthew 1:19 describes Joseph as a just man who was "faithful to the law." According to Jewish custom, Mary would have been listed in the ketubah (marriage contract) as a virgin. Being found pregnant before the final stage of marriage (nissuin) meant she appeared to have violated that agreement and could be accused of adultery—a capital offense under Deuteronomy 22:23-24. In such cases, the woman would be brought before the lesser Sanhedrin, a court of 23 judges.

While many assume Mary would have been executed for adultery, that outcome was highly unlikely—not because the law didn't apply, but because it required strict conditions: physical evidence and the testimony of two or three eyewitnesses. In Mary's case, there was no man involved, and therefore no witnesses to any alleged act of adultery.

It is also important to remember that under Jewish legal procedure, it was the witnesses, not the accused, who were interrogated (Deuteronomy 19:18). Which means Joseph himself would have been questioned and not Mary. Joseph had no physical proof and no corroborating witnesses, making any legal case against Mary impossible to uphold.

Another idea Christians have presented is that Joseph could have charged Mary with the law of Jealousy or the law of Sotah. This law is found in Numbers 5:11-31. Sota is the Hebrew word for unfaithful. The main reason Christians are in error by suggesting Joseph could have enacted the law of Sota is that this law did not apply to women who were betrothed. The Mishnah Sotah 2:1 and Talmud (Sotah 23b) explain that the ritual does not apply to a woman only betrothed (without nissuin), a woman divorced or widowed before drinking the waters, or other women not fully under the husband's authority in the marriage. This is because the ritual is tied to women who possessed a ketubah (marriage contract), cohabitation rights as a wife, and the husband's legal standing over her as a fully married woman. A betrothed woman possesses a ketubah, but she cannot cohabitate with her husband.

A Private Divorce?

Many Christian teachings conclude that Joseph was planning a "private divorce." This interpretation is based on the phrase in Matthew 1:19 that Joseph was "minded to put her away privily." However, this understanding relies on a mistranslation of the phrase "put away" as "divorce."

The idea of a secret or private divorce doesn't align with Jewish law. In first-century Judaism, all divorces were handled publicly in a tribunal court known as the Beit Din—the lowest legal court in Israel. This process required three judges, a scribe, and two non-family witnesses. Even if the reason for the divorce wasn't made public, the proceedings themselves were not secret.

Additionally, Mary lived in Nazareth (Luke 1:26), a small village with an estimated population of 300 to 500 people. In such a small community, news traveled quickly. It's likely the entire village attended Joseph and Mary's betrothal ceremony (erusin), and Mary would have begun using the only mikvah in Nazareth along with the other married women—further signaling her status. Since the Beit Din judges would have been locals from the same village, it would have been nearly impossible to carry out a divorce in complete secrecy.

Traditionally, a Jewish woman covers her hair once she enters the nissuin stage of marriage. If she becomes divorced or widowed, she is no longer obligated to cover her hair in the same way as a married woman. The Talmud (Ketubot 72a) bases hair covering on dat Yehudit — the Jewish standard of modesty for married women. Once a woman is no longer married, through divorce (get) or widowhood, she is released from these marital modesty requirements. In many traditional communities, widows and divorced women uncovered their hair, signaling that they were no longer under a husband's authority and were free to remarry (Deuteronomy 24:2).

Regarding Mary and Joseph, during their betrothal (kiddushin), Mary's hair would not yet have been covered. During the kiddushin stage, the woman remains at her father's house, so she is under the authority of the father and not the husband until after the nissuin. Mary would have received a token of betrothal — an object of value. Depending on local Galilean custom, this could have been a nose ring (Genesis 24:47; Ezekiel 16:11–12; Isaiah 3:21) or a finger ring. This token was an outward sign that Mary was legally betrothed. If the kiddushin were dissolved by divorce, the ring would be returned to the man, signaling publicly that she was no longer betrothed. This cultural practice debunks the idea of a "private divorce."

Joseph married (nissuin) Mary immediately following the angel's dream. Matthew 1:24 explains that Joseph "took Mary as his wife," while verse 25 clarifies that he did not consummate the marriage until after the birth of Jesus.

Matthew 1:24-25 (NLT)
24 When Joseph woke up, he did as the angel of the Lord commanded and took Mary as his wife.
25 But he did not have sexual relations with her until her son was born. And Joseph named him Jesus.

The Greek word apolyō is often mistranslated as "divorce," but it does not actually mean that. Apolyō simply means "to send away" or "to let go." For example, when Jesus dismissed the crowds in verses like Matthew 14:15, 14:22, 15:23, and 15:39, the word used is apolyō—yet clearly, He wasn't divorcing them.

If we insist that apolyō always means "divorce," we run into problems. For instance, in Mark 10:12, Jesus says, "If a woman divorces her husband and marries another, she commits adultery." But under Jewish law, a woman could not legally issue a divorce—only a man could. This suggests that apolyō is not referring to a formal legal divorce in this context, but rather to a woman separating from her husband without proper legal procedure. So, interpreting apolyō as "divorce" leads to confusion and misrepresents the original intent of the text.

Mark 10:12 (KJV)
And if a woman shall put away her husband, and be married to another, she committeth adultery.

In ancient Israel, women could not legally divorce their husbands. Under halakha (Jewish law), only men could initiate a divorce; the courts would not allow a woman to do so. This legal restriction is what gave rise to the ongoing agunah crisis—where women are left "chained" to husbands who refuse to grant them a divorce. This issue has existed since the time of Moses and still affects Jewish communities today.

We cannot rewrite historical and cultural realities to fit modern doctrines. If a woman were to "put away" (or send away) her husband and then marry another man without receiving a valid legal divorce (get), she would be committing adultery, since she would still be legally married to her first husband.

In Mark 10:12, when Jesus says, "If a woman divorces her husband and marries another, she commits adultery," He was not changing the law of Moses—He was affirming it. Jesus was not simply repeating the law in a general sense, but was likely referencing a well-known woman of that time who had acted outside the bounds of the law.

So, what was Joseph's plan? It was exactly as the scriptures describe. If we replace the phrase "put her away" with the actual meaning of the Greek word apolyō—"send away"—then the passage tells us that Joseph intended to send Mary away quietly. Scripture explicitly says that Joseph was "not willing to make her a public example," which is precisely what a legal charge of adultery or a formal divorce would have done.

The Hebrew Names Version Bible explains that Joseph "intended to put her away secretly." The Young's Literal Translation is the most accurate translation stating Joseph "did wish privately to send her away."

Matthew 1:19 (HNV)
Yosef, her husband, being a righteous man, and not willing to make her a public example intended to put her away secretly.

Matthew 1:19 (YLT)
and Joseph her husband being righteous, and not willing to make her an example , did wish privately to send her away.

At this point, Mary had just returned from the hill country of Judah, where she had stayed with her cousin Elisabeth for three months. If Joseph had planned to divorce her, he could have done so discreetly in another town, far from Nazareth, to avoid public shame. But instead of pursuing legal action, Joseph and Mary traveled together to Bethlehem for the census and taxation, further avoiding public exposure.

Importantly, all of this took place while Joseph and Mary were still in the kiddushin stage—the legal betrothal period, during which they were considered husband and wife but had not yet completed the final wedding ceremony (nissuin).

Luke 2:4-6 (KJV)
4. And Joseph also went up from Galilee, out of the city of Nazareth, into Judaea, unto the city of David, which is called Bethlehem; (because he was of the house and lineage of David:)
5. To be taxed with Mary his espoused wife, being great with child.
6. And so it was, that, while they were there, the days were accomplished that she should be delivered.

Mary and Joseph were still in the betrothal phase when they traveled to Bethlehem, though Matthew states that Joseph might have married Mary before the birth of Jesus (Matthew 1:24-25). After His birth, they did not immediately return to Nazareth. Instead, they traveled to Jerusalem to fulfill the requirement of circumcision, which was to be performed on the eighth day after birth (Luke 2:21). Following this, they returned to Bethlehem, where they were still living when the wise men visited (Matthew 2:7–8).

Soon after, Joseph received a warning in a dream instructing him to take Mary and Jesus to Egypt for their safety (Matthew 2:13–15). Scholars estimate that the family remained in Egypt for two to four years. After Herod's death, they returned to Israel and settled in the city of Nazareth (Matthew 2:21–23).

We later find Jesus still living in Nazareth at age twelve, when He traveled with His parents to Jerusalem for the Passover. It was during this trip that Jesus stayed behind in the temple, engaging with the teachers (Luke 2:41–50).

Several factors contributed to Israelite men abandoning their wives instead of granting them a formal divorce. One key factor—often overlooked in Christian teachings—was the dowry. In many Christian circles, the significance of the dowry has been dismissed or misunderstood, yet it played a crucial role in the legal and financial dynamics of marriage and divorce in ancient Israel.

The Dowry (*Nedunyah*)

The father's dowry is called a nedunyah. The dowry consisted of assets, a portion of the father's wealth, which belonged to the woman. The husband was given rights over his wife's assets, which fell under two categories (nedunyah and melog). The wife determined which category each asset belonged to.

Nedunyah Property

The first category is zon barzel property. Under this category, the husband took responsibility for her dowry (land, slaves, money, valuables, etc.) and had full control over it, virtually as his own property. Mishnah, Yevamot 7:1 explains that if these assets increased in value, he benefited, but he was also responsible for any loss in value. He was to return these assets to the wife at the end of the marriage, whether through divorce or death, and he was required to compensate her for any damages or losses.

Melog Property – Usufruct

Under the category of usufruct, these assets belonged to the wife, but the income generated belonged to the husband. If the assets increased in value, she benefited, but if they decreased in value, she suffered the loss.

The principal belonged to the wife, but the husband benefited from the income. For example, the land belonged to the woman, and the profit from the fruit would benefit the husband. However, the husband was not responsible for the losses to the assets.

The Husband's Obligations

The husband's obligations to the wife were nonnegotiable. These included providing food, clothing, and conjugal rights, as outlined in Exodus 21:10.

Exodus 21:10
If he take him another wife; her *food*, her *raiment*, and her *duty of marriage*, shall he not diminish.

He was also required to pay for his wife's medical expenses, provide ransom if she were taken captive, and cover her burial expenses. The ketubah also outlined inheritance. Male children inherited the **ketubah** even if their mother died before their father. Female children were to be supported by the mother's estate until they were betrothed or of age.

If the man were to divorce his wife, he would suffer a major financial blow by paying her ketubah and restoring her dowry. Additionally, the man would be responsible for any losses or depreciation of the woman's assets, depending on which category she selected. Furthermore, the man would lose the profits (usufruct) from her assets moving forward after the divorce. If the wife had the financial status of being dependent, the man also lost his wife's earnings or handiwork (ma'aseh yadeha). The Woman of Valor in Proverbs 31:31 is praised for "her deeds" or "her works," which would include her "handiwork" (ma'aseh yadeha). Therefore, instead of divorcing their wives, many men would abandon them.

Jewishencyclopedia.com defines an "agunah" as "a woman whose husband has either abandoned her or, being absent, has not been heard from for some time. Having no proof of her husband's death, or being without a bill of divorce from him, her status as a wife remains forever unchanged; for Jewish law does not admit the presumption of death from a prolonged absence merely, nor can a wife obtain a divorce from an absent husband."

From the woman's perspective, Jesus' statement would make little sense. If a man separates from his wife and she remarries, being an agunah, she would be in an adulterous marriage.

Matthew 5:32 (KJV)
But I say unto you, That whosoever shall put away his wife, saving for the cause of fornication, causeth her to commit adultery: and whosoever shall marry her that is divorced committeth adultery.

The Law of Moses prevented this situation from happening because the priest, under no circumstances, would marry a woman who was an agunah and did not have a get.

The major problem was that these laws did not apply to men; they had another option. Since a man could have multiple wives, he was not required to present a get to the priest in order to remarry. As a result, men would often abandon their wives, move to another area, and remarry. Their remarriage was lawful because the Law of Moses permitted men to have multiple wives.

Exodus 21:10 (KJV)
If he take him another [wife]; her food, her raiment, and her duty of marriage, shall he not diminish.

Exploiting this law allowed men to avoid divorcing their wives.

Permission by One Hundred Rabbis (*Heter Meah Rabbanim*)

Polygamy was eventually outlawed around 1000 AD. The Ashkenazic halachic authority, Rabbeinu Gershom of Mainz, is said to have issued four decrees through his court. His bans prohibited polygamy and prohibited a man from divorcing a woman without her consent. This ordinance was called cherem Rabbenu Gershom, the ban of Rabbenu Gershom.

Rabbi Gershom also enacted the heter mei'ah rabbanim, which is translated to mean "permission by one hundred rabbis." In situations where a woman was unable to receive a get due to illness, refused to receive a get, or ran away and the husband could not give her a get, rabbis would grant permission for the man to remarry. There were four requirements put in place to ensure that the heter mei'ah rabbanim was not abused.

The requirements were that "one hundred rabbis from at least three different countries must sign on to granting the husband permission to remarry. These rabbis must be scholars and may only grant permission after carefully investigating the details of the situation to ensure that the heter is not abused. They must also issue a get and place it with a third party, along with the money that had originally been promised to the first wife in the kesubah (ketubah)." This is a quote from the article "The Heter Meah Rabbonim – An Overview" by Rabbi Yair Hoffman. Eventually, leniency was granted with the heter mei'ah rabbanim, allowing men to exploit this ordinance, even as polygamy was outlawed.

The law of Jealousy (*Sota*)

Many Christians are familiar with the law of Jealousy (the law of Sota) but many are do not understand how this law worked. This law was for husbands who suspected their wives of adultery but lacked witnesses or concrete proof. Found in Numbers 5:11–31, it outlines the specific procedure the husband was to follow, including the grain offering he was required to bring and the ritual the priest would perform with the suspected woman. This public and sacred process gave God the opportunity to judge hidden sin and either confirm the woman's guilt or vindicate her innocence.

Numbers 5:11-16 (NLT)

11 And the LORD said to Moses,

12. "Give the following instructions to the people of Israel. "Suppose a man's wife goes astray, and she is unfaithful to her husband

13. and has sex with another man, but neither her husband nor anyone else knows about it. She has defiled herself, even though there was no witness and she was not caught in the act.

14. If her husband becomes jealous and is suspicious of his wife and needs to know whether or not she has defiled herself,

15. the husband must bring his wife to the priest. He must also bring an offering of two quarts of barley flour to be presented on her behalf. Do not mix it with olive oil or frankincense, for it is a jealousy offering--an offering to prove whether or not she is guilty.

16. "The priest will then present her to stand trial before the LORD.

Though many are familiar with the Sotah ritual—where a woman suspected of adultery drank bitter water—fewer understand the specific steps a husband was required to take before he could bring his wife to the priest. Suspicion alone was not sufficient. The law carefully protected against impulsive or baseless accusations. A man could not simply act on jealousy; there had to be a formal warning (kinui) issued in the presence of witnesses, forbidding his wife from being secluded with a particular man. Only if she then disobeyed and entered into seclusion (setirah) with that man—again, witnessed—could the process continue. Even then, the ritual did not condemn her to death. Rather, it was a divine test to determine guilt or innocence in a case where no human evidence existed.

In the Talmud, Sotah 2a explains - "MISHNA: With regard to one who issues a warning to his wife not to seclude herself with a particular man, so that if she does not heed his warning, she will assume the status of a woman suspected by her husband of having been unfaithful [sota], Rabbi Eliezer says: He issues a warning to her based on, i.e., in the presence of, two witnesses for the warning to be effective. If two witnesses were not present for the warning, she is not a sota even if two witnesses saw her seclusion with another man..." However, if husband had intercourse with her after he warned her but before she drank the water then the woman cannot be subjected to the Sotah ritual.

The Mishnah Sotah 2:1 and Talmud (Sotah 23b) explain that there are several cases when the ritual did not apply. This would be in the case of a betrothed woman (without a nissuin). It applies only to women who have completed the second stage of marriage (nissuin) and are fully married. The law explicitly states that a woman who has received a divorce—whether a complete, conditional, or partial get—cannot be subjected to the Sotah ritual. This also applies to a widowed woman. A "partial get" refers to a divorce process that was initiated but not fully completed, which requires a kosher sofer (ritually qualified scribe), valid witnesses, proper delivery by the husband, and acceptance by the wife. If any of these steps are incomplete, the woman remains halachically married, which could place her in the status of an agunah (a "chained" woman unable to remarry). Furthermore, the Sotah law could not be invoked if the woman was not fully under the husband's legal authority within the marriage. I will explain this final condition in more detail momentarily.

The Sotah ritual was tied to three essential criteria. First, the woman had to be in possession of a ketubah, the marriage contract that legally established the marital relationship. Second, the couple had to have cohabitation rights, something a betrothed woman (arusah) did not yet possess, as cohabitation was only permitted after the second stage of marriage, known as nissuin. Third, the husband had to have full legal standing over his wife.

There are several cases in which a husband did not have legal standing over his wife. In these cases, the man could not make jealousy-based claims to the priest. A betrothed woman could not be taken to the priest. A betrothed woman has gone through erusin (betrothal) but not nissuin (full marriage). She is legally his wife in name but could do not live together. The man does not yet have conjugal rights. He cannot invoke the Sotah ritual because her father is still her legal authority.

If a man married a woman improperly or illegally the man could not invoke the Sotah ritual. If a marriage is halachically invalid or incomplete, the husband lacks full legal standing. This applies to a woman who married without proper kiddushin (betrothal). If a man lives with a woman without formal kiddushin (e.g. common-law marriage), he has no halachic rights over her.

A woman in a forbidden marriage (issur lav or kareit). If the marriage violates Torah law (e.g., a kohen marries a divorcee), it may be considered invalid or limited, and the man may not have the legal standing of a full husband.

If a man married a minor who was given in marriage by her mother or brothers, and not by her father, he could not invoke the Sotah law. According to Halacha, only a father has the legal authority to give a minor daughter in marriage with full halachic effect. Any marriage arranged by others (such as her mother or brothers) is considered conditional, and the girl has the right to annul it through mi'un (refusal) when she reaches the age of maturity. Until the girl comes of age, the husband lacks full halachic standing over her.

Under Jewish law, a female is considered a na'arah—a young woman— between the ages of 12 and 12½. During this stage, she is still under her father's legal authority but possesses greater personal legal standing. Her consent is required for marriage, though paternal jurisdiction still applies. Once a girl reaches the status of bogeret—an adult woman at 12½ years old and onward—she is regarded as fully mature and independent in Halacha. At that point, she can accept a kiddushin (marriage proposal) on her own, without requiring her father's consent or involvement.

The husband could not invoke the Sota law on a wife who is separated but not divorced. If a man separates from his wife but hasn't given her a get

(Jewish divorce), he may lose certain rights, depending on how long the separation has lasted or the terms involved. Sotah does not apply once divorce has occurred or is pending, because the full legal marital relationship has ended.

A widow whose husband died without children is bound to his brother through the obligation of levirate marriage (yibbum), as commanded in Deuteronomy 25:5–10. Until this obligation is resolved, the brother cannot invoke the Sotah law upon the widow (yevamah). The Sotah ritual is inapplicable until either yibbum (levirate marriage) is performed, or the chalitzah (release ceremony) is completed if yibbum is not desired.

Although the widow is prohibited from marrying another man until after chalitzah, the deceased husband's brother does not have full halachic authority over her during this interim period. His standing is limited; the marital bond (zika) that connects them is potential, not yet actualized through marriage, and thus insufficient to establish the legal conditions required for invoking the Sotah process.

THE *AGUNAH* CRISIS IN MODERN TIME

Jewish law requires a divorced couple to go through the Beit Din (the rabbinical court) for a divorce, even today. While the couple may get divorced through the civil court of the country in which they reside, they are still considered married in the eyes of the Jewish court until the woman receives her get. Jewish men, not needing a get, have used civil courts to divorce and then remarry, while Jewish women are left waiting for their get to move on or remarry.

This issue in the Jewish community is referred to as "The Agunah Crisis," a long-standing problem that dates back to before the time of Jesus. Jewish men have exploited the law of polygamy or, later, the ordinance of heter mei'ah rabbanim to free themselves to remarry. Men who refuse to grant their wives a get are called "get refusers." Public shaming, bans from synagogues, and social and business ostracism are just some of the measures taken to help free women who are agunah. Many organizations are dedicated to securing a get for trapped women. In some cases, extreme measures, including violence, have been used. In 2013, the FBI conducted a sting operation against a New York divorce coercion gang that kidnapped and tortured Jewish men in the New York metropolitan area, forcing them to grant their wives religious divorces (gittin). The Brooklyn rabbi, Mendel Epstein, called "The Prodfather" for using a cattle prod on his victims, was sentenced to 10 years in prison, with his accomplices receiving varying sentences. According to Rabbi Epstein, he was paid $70,000 for his services.

An internet search will reveal many organizations working to free Jewish women from their state of agunah. A search on the social media platform Instagram using hashtags like #getrefuser or #agunah will show many women (and also men) who are trapped in their marriages.

Get refusal is viewed by many as a form of spousal abuse. Men use it to assert power and control over their former wives. Men will demand money, assets, certain unfair benefits, or even custody of the children in exchange for providing the get. If a Jewish woman chooses to remarry without her get, her marriage is considered illegal by the Jewish court, and her children may be ostracized from the faith and community as mamzer (illegitimate).

An excellent article on the Agunah Crisis can be found at Jwa.org, titled "Agunot" by Shulamit S. Magnus. It explains the Jewish laws, the agunah crisis, and how Jewish women are extorted by their husbands. The article states, "A reported one-third of Israeli women experience some form of extortion to receive a get." The Editors of the Jewish Week reported in 2011, "In Israel, estimates of 10,000 agunot have been reported by the Wall Street Journal." The Chief Rabbinate still keeps "mamzer lists," as they did during the time of Jesus. The Chief Rabbinate stated that he "refuses to marry such people."

The Times of Israel has an article titled, "Longest-jailed Israeli divorce-refuser freed after 19 years," written by Marissa Newman. A man was incarcerated for over 19 years for refusing to grant his wife a divorce. Meir Gorodetsky chose to remain in jail rather than grant his wife a divorce, becoming the first man in Israel's history to be charged criminally for his refusal. "In June 2018, a private Orthodox rabbinical court, in a dramatic ruling, annulled the Gorodetsky nuptials." Tzviya Gorodetsky's 23-year battle finally came to an end.

Another insightful article is "Rabbinical court imposes million-shekel ($272,000) divorce payment on husband, citing ketubah" by Toi Staff (TimesofIsrael.com), written in May 2024. Ohad Hoffman, a lawyer specializing in family and inheritance issues, quoted by Israel's N12 news site, stated, "This judgment reflects the court's approach to more strongly protect women. When it is proven for sure that fault for the divorce lies with the man, it is the woman's right to collect the sum that she is entitled to, including the amount specified in the ketubah."

In addition to the men in Israel exploiting the loophole in the law by abandoning their wives, there was an even bigger problem in Israel during Jesus' time.

ANNULLED DIVORCES/ DIVORCE CANCELLATION AND FAKE BILL OF DIVORCEMENTS

Dr. Judith Hauptman, Rabbi Phillip R. Alstat Professor of Talmud at the Jewish Theological Seminary of America, teaches an online course entitled Women in Rabbinic Literature. An article on jewishvirtuallibrary. org titled "Issues in Jewish Ethics: Annulment of Marriage" by Judith Hauptman reveals a significant problem that occurred in Israel during Jesus' time. This issue was so widespread that the rabbinical court had to pass a law to address and resolve it.

People began appointing agents to perform legal acts in court on their behalf. In the article "Kiddushin, Daf Mem Aleph, Part 2" by the Fuchsberg Center (Fuchsbergcenter.org), it explains that "the rabbis derive the notion that a person can appoint an agent who can perform acts of legal consequence on his/her behalf" from Deuteronomy 24:1.

"From where do we know [the principle of] agency? As it was taught: [Then he shall write her a bill of divorcement . . .] and he shall send [her out of his house] (Deuteronomy 24:1): this teaches that he may appoint an agent; then she shall send: this teaches that she may appoint an agent; then he shall send, then he shall send her: this teaches that the agent can appoint an agent."

In other words, the "he" in Deuteronomy 24:1 did not specifically have to be the husband; it could be a representative. If the man could have an agent to represent him, then the woman could also have an agent to represent her.

Men began using agents for various legal matters, including delivering gets (bills of divorce) to their wives. However, the husband had the right to render the bill of divorce void. So, the husband would send an agent to deliver the get to the woman, but then, Dr. Hauptman explains, the man "would convene a court elsewhere and render the bill of divorce void in the presence of the court before it reached his wife." The men would annul their divorce without informing their wives.

Mishnah Gittin 4:2 further explains that Rabban Gamaliel the Elder, who was the president (nasi) of the Sanhedrin, the supreme Jewish Court, instituted an ordinance in response to this problem. A law was passed prohibiting men from doing this "in order to repair the social order Mipnei Tikkun Ha-Olam" which is translated "one should not do this, for the betterment of the world".

The article by Dr. Hauptman explains that the restriction required the man to inform his wife if he had canceled the get he sent her. Rabban Gamaliel explained, "Allowing a husband to cancel a get after it was drawn up and dispatched but before it was delivered to her was reasonable, but it became unreasonable and unfair if he were not required to inform his wife of the cancellation."

"Gamaliel repaired the social order, which means, in this case, improving the lot of women and children. Until that time, a woman could receive a get that looked perfectly valid, remarry, and only afterward, most likely by chance, find out that her husband had canceled it. In such a case, her second union would be adulterous, and the children of that union would be mamzerim."

The main purpose of the law was to address another problem: "the unfairness of delivering to a wife a get that looks perfectly valid, only to have her discover at a later date that it was a worthless piece of paper."

Additionally, Rabban Gamaliel instituted that a get should list all names by which the husband and wife are commonly known. The Gemara explains that initially, the husband would change both his name and her name from the names by which they were known where they formerly lived to the names by which they were known where the bill of divorce was written and would include the name of his city and the name of her city. One was not required to list all of the names by which the husband and wife were known, but only the names in the place where the bill of divorce was being written. Rabban Gamaliel the Elder instituted that the scribe should write in the bill of divorce: "The man so-and-so, and any other name that he has, and: The woman so-and-so, and any other name that she has."

"The reason for this ordinance was for the betterment of the world, as perhaps the people of a different city would not recognize the name written in the bill of divorce and would claim that this bill of divorce does not belong to her."

This unethical practice of men annulling their divorces and not informing their wives led to women unknowingly entering adulterous marriages. The woman would have received a get, which would have allowed the priest to remarry her; however, the get would later be deemed invalid by the court. The man who married her would be viewed as an adulterer by the court, and the couple would be required to divorce, with the woman still legally married to her former husband. An Israelite woman with an invalid bill of divorce would have only been "put away" and would not have been legally divorced by her husband. In Israel, an Israelite with a ketubah was required by law to have a valid bill of divorce to remarry, unlike a concubine who could simply be "put away."

When we examine Jesus' statement regarding remarriage, we can see how his words align with the law passed by Gamaliel and the Sanhedrin, and how they actually reinforce the law of Moses.

Matthew 5:32
(Young's Literal Translation) but I -- I say to you, that whoever
may put away his wife, save for the matter of whoredom, doth
make her to commit adultery; and whoever may marry her who
hath been put away doth commit adultery.

Matthew 19:9
(Young's Literal Translation) And I say to you, that, whoever may
put away his wife, if not for whoredom, and may marry another,
doth commit adultery; and he who did marry her that hath been
put away, doth commit adultery.

Jesus was not saying it was forbidden to marry a divorced woman. He
stated that it was forbidden to marry a woman who was not legally divorced
from her husband.

Name Changes in the Bible (Torah)

Gamaliel had to address the issue of people having multiple names
when it came to the bill of divorce. This was done to resolve the problem of
claims that the bill of divorce did not belong to the woman. Shlomo Chaim
Kesselman (chabad.org) explains that name changes were common in
ancient Israel, especially when a person's role or status changed. For
example, kings and other leaders often took on new names when they
became powerful. Names in biblical times were often based on a person's
birth circumstances, a situation, an event, or a personal characteristic.
They could also be reminiscent of animal or plant names.

Some examples of name changes in the Bible include: Jacob became
Israel; Joseph became Zaphenath-paneah; Hosea became Joshua; Eliakim
and Mattaniah became Jehoiakim and Zedekiah, respectively; Hadassah
became Esther; Peter's name was Simon (Matthew 10:2) and also Cephas
(John 1:42). There are many others throughout scripture.

Michal, the daughter of Saul and wife of David, had her name changed
to Eglah (heifer), which means "heifer" because she died during childbirth,

bleating like a cow. This would be a name reminiscent of an animal. Esau was named so because he was hairy at birth (Genesis 25:25). Esau means "hairy," a name based on a personal characteristic.

Esther's birth name was Hadassah, which means myrtle, a fragrant evergreen shrub known for its aromatic leaves and white or pink flowers, which produce dark berries. This would be a name reminiscent of plant names.

Name changes in Israel were common. If the court viewed the woman's get as not belonging to her, she could potentially become an agunah and never be permitted to remarry, remaining stuck in that status for life.

Who is Rabban Gamaliel?

Rabban Gamaliel was responsible for passing the restrictions on the law requiring the woman to be informed of an annulled get and requiring all known names to be included on the get. He is also called Gamaliel the Elder. He was the grandson of the renowned sage Hillel and the mentor to the Apostle Paul. He was one of the last presidents of Israel before the Temple was destroyed in the 1st century CE. He is mentioned in the scriptures in Acts 5:34 and Acts 22:3.

Acts 22:3 (KJV)
I am verily a man [which am] a Jew, born in Tarsus, [a city] in Cilicia, yet brought up in this city at the feet of Gamaliel, [and] taught according to the perfect manner of the law of the fathers, and was zealous toward God, as ye all are this day.

Gamaliel was born sometime before Jesus' birth and died in 52 AD. I highlight Gamaliel's name in the scriptures to show that his ordinance regarding divorce was passed during the time of Jesus' teaching. This means this problem was occurring in Israel well before Jesus and the Sanhedrin saw the need to address it. Men were purposely deceiving their wives by annulling the divorce and not informing them, or by sending invalid gets, causing their wives to enter into adulterous marriages.

We can now see why Jesus repeatedly made the statement that if they put away their wives and their wives married another man, it was adultery. Through deception, the women in Israel were entering into adulterous marriages, believing their divorces were legal.

EXCEPT FOR FORNICATION

Matthew 5:32 (KJV)
But I say unto you, That whosoever shall put away his wife, *saving for the cause of fornication*, causeth her to commit adultery: and whosoever shall marry her that is divorced committeth adultery.

Christians have commonly and confidently taught that Jesus said adultery was the exception to divorce. As a result, it has been accepted that adultery is the only just cause for divorce. One major error in this teaching is that Jesus never mentioned adultery; He specifically said fornication.

Christians typically define fornication as referring exclusively to sexual activity before marriage, while adultery involves married couples. Consequently, some Christians conclude that Jesus was speaking about single people. The first problem with this interpretation is that Jesus said, "Whosoever shall put away his wife..." Clearly, Jesus is talking about a married couple. To make sense of this, the Christian teaching suggests that this statement refers to the betrothal period, which under Jewish law required a divorce to dissolve the marriage agreement. That part is true; however, it is often taught that Jesus restricted divorce solely to the betrothal phase of the relationship, implying that divorce is not permitted after the final phase of marriage. If this teaching were accurate, it would mean that Jesus completely altered the entire Jewish system of marriage and divorce. Under Jewish law, a betrothed woman was no longer considered single, but was already regarded as a married woman.

Jesus clearly quoted the law of Moses in Matthew 5:31.

Matthew 5:31 (KJV)
It hath been said, Whosoever shall put away his wife, let him give her a writing of divorcement:

This law is found in Deuteronomy 24:1.

Deuteronomy 24:1 (KJV)
When a man hath taken a wife, and married her, and it come to pass that she find no favour in his eyes, because he hath found some uncleanness in her: then let him write her a bill of divorcement, and give [it] in her hand, and send her out of his house.

According to the law of Moses, divorce was required for both couples that were betrothed and those who were married. The couple could not live together until the last phase, the nissuin, was completed, as seen in Deuteronomy 24:1. The law states that the man had "taken a wife and married her." This refers to a couple that has completed the two stages of a Jewish wedding: betrothal (kiddushin) and marriage (nissuin). The woman could not live in the man's house until after the nissuin, not during the kiddushin. The law of Moses does not restrict the requirement for a legal divorce to only the betrothal stage.

If Jesus did not change or abolish the law, as He stated in Matthew 5:17, then we must reconsider what Jesus is saying. His statement cannot violate the law of Moses in any way.

Regarding single people engaging in sexual activity, it was not viewed as "fornication" in Israel as it is in American culture. The Jewish court viewed adultery as a crime, and there were also laws against fornication as it would be defined in American culture. What was the penalty for fornication?

If a man lay with a woman who was not betrothed, he was required to marry her. The father had the right to disapprove of the marriage. In these cases, the court required the man to pay the father punitive damages, which was the mōhar, the bride price for her virginity.

Exodus 22:16-17 (KJV)
16. And if a man entice a maid that is not betrothed, and lie with her, he shall surely endow her to be his wife.
17. If her father utterly refuse to give her unto him, he shall pay money according to the dowry [mōhar] of virgins.

In addition, if the man married the woman whose virginity he took before they became betrothed, he lost his right to divorce her forever (Deuteronomy 22:29). The father of the woman did have the right to object to the marriage.

In Israel, once the couple was engaged, the woman's status changed; she was no longer viewed as single. Thus, the Christian teaching violates the law of Moses and Jewish customs. A betrothed woman was viewed as married and not single in the eyes of the law. If a man were to touch a betrothed woman he would be put to death, the same as a married woman (Deuteronomy 22:25-27). Once a woman became betrothed (kiddushin), she could not engage in consensual sexual activity outside of marriage. The concept of kiddushin is that the woman was made "holy" and set apart (sanctified). This is a Jewish truth upon which Christian doctrine is built. The bride of Christ, the Church, has been made holy and set apart for Christ.

1 Thessalonians 4:3 (KJV)
For this is the will of God, *[even] your sanctification*, that ye should abstain from fornication:

The word kiddushin means "holiness." After the woman signed the marriage agreement (the ketubah) and the betrothal ceremony (also known as erusin) had occurred, she was off-limits to all men, including the bridegroom. For her to engage in consensual sex with another man at this point, both she and the man she lay with would be put to death (Deuteronomy 22:23-24). If a man lay with a woman who was betrothed and it was not consensual, only the man was put to death (Deuteronomy 22:25).

So, for Christians to teach that divorce could only occur for "fornication", limiting divorce to before the wedding ceremony, alters and violates the law of Moses and Jewish customs.

The problem lies in how the Church defines the word porneia (fornication). The word porneia is a broad term that has evolved over time. Esau was described as a fornicator in Hebrews 12:16, and yet there is no mention of any physical activity with a woman. Esau, according to Scriptures, was a fornicator for selling his birthright for one morsel of meat.

The prophets use this term metaphorically to describe idolatry as spiritual adultery. The word porneia is frequently used in the New Testament in relation to idolatry. It is connected to acts of idolatry, which included idols, foods sacrificed to idols, and pagan worship, which often involved immoral sexual acts in the temple of a false god (see Acts 15:20, Acts 15:29, Rev. 2:14, Rev. 2:20).

Some Christians argue that idolatry was the exception and that divorce was limited to cases where a man's wife became involved in idolatry. The major problem with this argument is that, like adultery, idolatry was a capital crime. Idolatry was punishable by death (see Leviticus 20:2, Deuteronomy 13:7-19, Deuteronomy 17:2-7).

There is an explanation that does not violate the law of Moses. Paul uses the word porneia and gives us a very specific example of fornication. Paul describes a man in the church of Corinth who was involved with his stepmother.

1 Corinthians 5:1 (KJV)
It is reported commonly [that there is] *fornication (porneia)* among you, and such fornication as is not so much as named among the Gentiles, that one should have his father's wife.

Leviticus 18 lists unions that were considered incestuous under the law of Moses. These are forbidden sexual practices (unlawful sexual relations) in Israel. The relationship Paul described would be considered an incestuous union according to the law of Moses. Such relationships were viewed as a crime by the Jewish court, and the punishments included death, exile, impurity, and barrenness (see Leviticus 20).

In the 1st-century Jewish context, the Greek word porneia—often translated as "fornication"—commonly referred to unlawful sexual unions, including incestuous marriages, not merely premarital sex. The Jewish historian Josephus (Antiquities 15.259–260) uses porneia to describe Herod Antipas' marriage to Herodias, his brother's wife, which Jewish law considered incest. Rabbinic writings, such as the Mishnah and Talmud (e.g., Yevamot, Kiddushin, Sanhedrin), list forbidden marriages based on Leviticus 18, and sexual relations within these unions were labeled as "fornication" or "sexual immorality." The Qumran community (Dead Sea Scrolls) likewise interpreted the Hebrew term zanut ("fornication") as violations of Levitical sexual laws, especially incest, as seen in the Damascus Document (CD 4:20–5:11). Strong's Lexicon confirms that porneia encompasses harlotry, adultery, and incest, and can also be used figuratively for idolatry. In the biblical world, incest was considered part of the broader category of porneia, not a separate category.

Paul pointed out that such a union was not even named among the Gentiles.

1 Corinthians 5:1 (KJV)
It is reported commonly [that there is] fornication among you, and
such fornication as is not so much as named among the
Gentiles, that one should have his father's wife.

This statement implies that such a union was also unlawful in Rome, and this conclusion is accurate. Roman law strictly prohibited marriage between a man and his stepmother. Like Jewish law, this was considered incestuous and was forbidden under the concept of "connubium," which defined who could legally marry whom under Roman law.

Marriage in Roman Law by Andrew T. Bierkan, Charles P. Sherman, Emile Stocquart, and Jur. in The Yale Law Journal, Vol. 16, No. 5 (Mar. 1907), pp. 306, explains what was considered an incestuous union: "Whoever marries a relative in the direct line renders himself guilty of incest, according to the jus gentium. Anyone who marries a relative in a collateral line, contrary to an express prohibition of the law, or even a relative by marriage, with whom he is forbidden to marry..."

In Rome, the punishment for the crime of an incestuous marriage varied depending on whether the individuals were related by a direct line, collateral kin, or relation by adoption. Such punishments included death, deportation, fines, or changes in social status.

Therefore, Jesus explained that the exception for divorce was unlawful marriages (fornication). He was not creating "new laws." The same laws applied in Israel as in Rome (though the penalties differed). These were marriages viewed as unlawful from the beginning and were therefore invalid according to the law, meaning no divorce was required.

Marriage in Roman Law by Andrew T. Bierkan, Charles P. Sherman, Emile Stocquart, and Jur. in The Yale Law Journal, Vol. 16, No. 5 (Mar. 1907), pp. 124, explains that an incestuous marriage "expressly prohibited in the eighteenth chapter of Leviticus, were regarded as a nullity, requiring no formal divorce."

We can see in the scriptures where divorce laws were enforced. In Ezra 10:16-17, although this was not a case of incest, we find marriages being given the status of "nullity." Over 100 men are named whom God required to "put away" their wives. Many believe this was because they married foreign women (Ezra 10:11), which is partially true. These women were from nations God forbade the Israelites to marry. However, in addition, these women never became converts; they maintained their lifestyle, culture, and religious practices. So, when God required the men to "put away" their wives and children (Ezra 10:44) born from these unions, no formal divorce was required. These women would not have had a ketubah, as a Jewish court would not have viewed such marriages as lawful, so no get would have been issued. Bill of Divorcements were only required for women with a ketubah, a legally binding marriage agreement.

In Israel, certain unlawful marriages did not require a formal divorce by the court. In these cases, the Jewish court viewed the betrothal as invalid, meaning the kiddushin never took effect. While both incestuous and adulterous marriages were prohibited by Jewish law, the legal consequences differed. However, children born from either of these unions were regarded as mamzerim (bastards).

Jewishvirtuallibrary.org, in its section on "Prohibited Marriages," explains the "Legal Consequences of Prohibited Marriages." It cites "Shulchan Arukh, Even HaEzer 15:1" and "Shulchan Arukh, Even HaEzer 44:6": "So far as the parties themselves are concerned, no legal consequences at all attach to a marriage that is forbidden as (incestuous) according to Pentateuchal law, and there is therefore no need for them to be divorced (Sh. Ar., EH 15:1 and Sh. Ar., EH 44:6); their children will be mamzerim. Only a marriage of a married woman to another man, although invalid, requires that the woman obtain a divorce not only from her husband but also from the paramour (see *Divorce; *Bigamy; *Agunah)."

Under U.S. law, unlawful marriages are annulled. An annulled marriage does not require a formal divorce. When a marriage is annulled, the court does not issue a "divorce decree" because an annulment legally declares that the marriage was never valid in the first place. In such cases, the court issues an "annulment decree," essentially stating that the marriage never existed.

Matthew 5:32 (KJV)
But I say unto you, That whosoever shall put away his wife, saving
for the cause of fornication, causeth her to commit adultery: and
whosoever shall marry her that is divorced committeth adultery.

So, Jesus never stated that the only cause for a divorce was fornication. In Jewish law, porneía (as used in 1st century Greek) corresponded to forbidden sexual unions. Jesus was discussing marital unions as seen by the court. He stated that if a man separated from his wife, except in the cases where the marriage was never valid and no legal divorce was needed, the wife remained a married woman and needed a valid divorce. And if someone were to marry this separated woman, then they would be committing adultery. Jesus was teaching the law of Moses. Jesus was describing forbidden marriages: the crime (illegal act) of bigamy (Deuteronomy 23:2) and incestuous marriages (Leviticus 18:6-18).

In the scripture, we find two incestuous relationships, both of which occurred before the law of Moses was established. The scripture tells us that there was sin before the law, but it was not counted as sin because there was no law yet to break (Romans 5:13). Therefore, there were no legal penalties, such as death, flogging, imprisonment, or fines. However, these sins did not go unchecked.

In Genesis 9:22, Ham, the son of Noah, "saw the nakedness of his father." Many have erroneously taught that Noah had an immoral relationship with his son. However, the term "nakedness of the father" is used in Leviticus 18 to describe the father's wife. Therefore, Ham had relations with his mother, not his father. This resulted in the birth of Canaan.

Genesis 9:18 (KJV)

And the sons of Noah, that went forth of the ark, were Shem, and **Ham**, and Japheth: ***and Ham is the father of Canaan***.

In Genesis 35:22, Reuben, the son of Jacob, lay with his stepmother, Bilhah. Not only did Reuben lie with his father's wife, but Bilhah was also his mother Leah's half-sister. When Leah and Rachel married Jacob, they were both given handmaidens by their father Laban. Bilhah and Zilpah were Leah and Rachel's half-sisters. Reuben would have been guilty of violating Leviticus 18:8 and 18:13; however, since the law of Moses had not yet been established, Reuben was not charged with a sin (Romans 5:13). Nevertheless, Reuben's actions did not go unpunished, as seen in the blessing Jacob prophesied over his first-born son. Jacob prophesied that the tribe of Reuben would not excel, and indeed, that tribe did not surpass Judah or Levi, as those two tribes became exalted above the rest.

Genesis 49:3-4 (NIV)

3. "Reuben, you are my firstborn, my might, the first sign of my strength, excelling in honor, excelling in power.

4. Turbulent as the waters, *you will no longer excel, for you went up onto your father's bed, onto my couch and defiled it*.

In the case of Ham, the child Canaan was cursed by Noah.

Genesis 9:25 (KJV) And he said, **Cursed be Canaan**; a servant of servants shall he be unto his brethren.

This curse does not imply that Canaan experienced a life of difficulties himself, but rather that it applied to his descendants. Canaan became the father of the Canaanites, and Abraham did not allow Isaac to marry a daughter of the Canaanites. Once the nation of Israel was established, the law of Moses forbade Israelites from marrying individuals from seven nations, which included the Canaanites (Deuteronomy 7:1-6).

In the stories of Reuben and Ham, we see the consequences fall upon their children or their bloodline. This is also consistent with the structure of the law of Moses. A child born from a forbidden marriage would take on a status such as mamzer or chalalah, being barred from the congregation or the priesthood due to the sin of their parents. This aligns with the broader law of sin, as we have all sinned and fallen short of the glory of God because of Adam's sin in the garden. We are the descendants of Adam.

Romans 5:12

Wherefore, *as by one man sin entered into the world*, and death by sin; and so death passed upon all men, *for that all have sinned*:

The sins of the father often affect the children, as seen with many kings who turned away from God, causing the consequences of their decisions to impact their offspring. However, the sins of the father are not visited upon those who choose righteousness, as explained in Ezekiel 18.

Would Jesus' statement, "except in the case of fornication" — or more accurately, "except in the case of an incestuous marriage" — have been relevant to His audience during the Sermon on the Mount? Yes, but not because incestuous marriages were widespread. In fact, such unions were rare in Israel due to the clear prohibitions in the Law (Leviticus 18). However, one high-profile case was fresh in the public's mind: King Herod's unlawful marriage to his brother Philip's wife (Matthew 14:3), which violated Leviticus 18:6 and 18:16. John the Baptist, Jesus' cousin, publicly condemned this union. So, while Jesus wasn't addressing a common problem, He was speaking to a notorious and well-known example of unlawful marriage that His audience would have clearly recognized.

Valid Forbidden Unions and Invalid Forbidden Unions:

Under Jewish law (Halacha), a Get (bill of divorcement) is always required to terminate a marriage initiated through kiddushin (betrothal) and nissuin (marital cohabitation). However, there are cases where a get is not required to end a marriage. Forbidden marriages in Israel were viewed as valid and invalid. If the marriage was technically valid under Jewish law, a get was necessary to end it. If the marriage was considered void from the outset (ein kiddushin tofsin), then no valid marriage exists, and a get is not required.

1. Marriage Between a Jew and a Non-Jew Is Invalid in Halacha:

According to Torah law (Deuteronomy 7:3-4) and rabbinic tradition, a marriage between a Jewish person and a non-Jew is prohibited and has no legal standing as a valid marriage under Halacha. This is not just a prohibition; it means that no halachic kiddushin (betrothal) takes place, and therefore, the union lacks halachic marital status. Since there was never a valid halachic marriage, no Get is required to dissolve the relationship. The child of a Jewish mother and a non-Jewish father is considered Jewish. The child of a non-Jewish mother and a Jewish father is considered non-Jewish (Gentile) and would need a halachic conversion to be considered Jewish.

Once a person converts to Judaism according to Halachic standards (with immersion, circumcision for males, and acceptance of mitzvot before a valid Beit Din), they are considered fully Jewish in every respect. A convert is treated as any other Jew regarding marriage, divorce, and all other religious obligations. A get (bill of divorce) is required if a Jew marries a convert to Judaism (a ger/gerah tzedek) and they later seek to divorce.

2. Kiddushin by Error or Under False Pretenses (Mekach Ta'ut)

If the marriage was entered into under deception, coercion, or significant misinformation about essential aspects (e.g., hidden physical defects, infertility, disqualifying lineage), the marriage may be considered void ab initio (invalid from the start). In such cases, the court can rule that the kiddushin was never halachically valid, and no get is required.

3. Marriages Not Formalized by Halacha

If a couple never underwent a halachic kiddushin (betrothal)—meaning they did not follow the formal legal process of marriage (e.g., ring under witnesses, chuppah)—their union is not a binding halachic marriage. Therefore, separation would not require a get.

4. Incestuous Marriage (invalid)

An incestuous marriage, prohibited by Torah law according to Leviticus 18, is an invalid forbidden union. The marriage is considered void from the outset. Since no valid marriage exists halakhically, a get is not required. However, rabbinic courts often still require a formal separation process to prevent confusion over status.

5. Mamzer (valid)

A Jew who marries a mamzer enters a valid, though restricted, union. Because the marriage is halakhically binding, if they divorce, a get is required to dissolve it (Mishnah Kiddushin 3:12; Shulchan Aruch, Even HaEzer 4:13). A mamzer is prohibited from marrying into the general community of Israel but may lawfully marry either another mamzer or a convert (Deuteronomy 23:3; Kiddushin 73a).

A mamzer is a child born from a forbidden sexual union, specifically adultery or incest. An adulterous union occurs when a woman's first marriage is still binding, yet she enters a second, unlawful marriage. Any children born from this second union are considered mamzerim, regarded as illegitimate under Jewish law. An incestuous union occurs when the kinship between a man and a woman is too close, as defined in Leviticus 18. A mamzer is not a child of an unmarried couple (fornication), nor is the child of a Jew and a non-Jew considered a mamzer.

6. Kohen - marriage to a divorcee, widow, etc. (valid)

A kohen is forbidden to marry a divorcee, widowed, convert, zonah (harlot), or chalalah, as stated in Leviticus 21:7. While such marriages are prohibited, they are nevertheless halakhically valid and therefore require a **get** to be dissolved (Mishnah Kiddushin 3:12; Shulchan Aruch, Even HaEzer 6:1). In contrast to an Israelite, who may remarry his divorced wife provided she has not married another man in the meantime (Deuteronomy 24:1–4), a kohen is permanently barred from remarrying his divorced wife under any circumstance (Mishnah Sotah 5:1; Rambam, Hilkhot Issurei Biah 1:7). Should a kohen enter a forbidden marriage, the children of that union are classified as chalalim: sons are disqualified from priestly service, and daughters are prohibited from marrying kohanim (Mishnah Kiddushin 4:1; Shulchan Aruch, Even HaEzer 7:17). However, if the woman was already pregnant from a permitted union at the time of the marriage, the child does not bear the status of chalal, since conception did not result from the forbidden relationship (Yevamot 49a; Tosafot ad loc.) — the child was not conceived in sin (lo ba mi-tipat aveirah).

7. Death of a Spouse

If one spouse dies, the marriage is naturally dissolved, and no get is required. However, halitzah (levirate release ceremony) may be required if the husband dies childless, to release the widow from yibbum (levirate marriage obligation). The widow is not permitted to marry anyone else. She is bound to the brother-in-law (as if "engaged") due to the yibbum obligation. This status is called zekukah le-yibbum (bound for levirate marriage). After the halitzah is performed, she is released from the levirate bond. She is free to marry whomever she wishes, except for certain close relatives or a Kohen (priests) - in some cases.

A get is always required to end a valid Jewish marriage. However, if the marriage was never valid to begin with (invalid kiddushin, forbidden unions, fraudulent circumstances), a get may not be required because the marriage is considered null and void under Halacha.

PAUL'S ARGUMENTS DO NOT CONTRADICT THE LAW

There are several passages from the Apostle Paul that people refer to when making arguments about divorce and remarriage. As we will see, Paul's teachings do not violate the law of Moses.

Romans 7 (Apothnēskō)

In Romans 7, Paul is not discussing marriage, divorce, or remarriage. He is using marriage as an analogy to make his point. His argument is that, through our death with Christ, we are freed from the first covenant, enabling us to enter into a new covenant with Jesus Christ.

> Romans 7:4 (NLT)
> So, my dear brothers and sisters, ***this is the point***: You died to the power+ of the law when you died with Christ. And now you are united with the one who was raised from the dead. As a result, we can produce a harvest of good deeds for God.

In verse one, Paul begins by addressing those who are familiar with the law. The marriage laws are outlined in Deuteronomy 24:1-4. However, many teach a version of the law that contradicts the law of Moses. They argue that remarriage is only permissible once a spouse dies, yet Deuteronomy 24:3 states that a woman can remarry after either being divorced or widowed.

Paul starts his argument by emphasizing that the law no longer has power over a person once they die. After death, there are no further legal consequences for the deceased.

Romans 7:1 (KJV)
Know ye not, brethren, (for I speak to them that know the law,)
how that the law hath dominion over a man as long as he liveth?

Paul then provides an illustration for his point by using marriage laws in Israel.

Romans 7:2-3 (KJV)
2. For the woman which hath an husband is bound by the law to
[her] husband so long as he liveth; but if the husband be dead, she
is loosed from the law of [her] husband.
3. So then if, while [her] husband liveth, she be married to another
man, she shall be called an adulteress: but if her husband be dead,
she is free from that law; so that she is no adulteress, though she be
married to another man.

Paul describes a situation where a woman enters into a second marriage while her first marriage still exists. Notably, Paul does not mention divorce in this passage. This passage is not about divorce. Rather, Paul uses this example to explain how we are freed from the first covenant. We are not divorced from the law; we died to the law.

However, those who argue that this passage states you can only remarry once your spouse has died overlook a crucial detail. The Greek language has several words for "dead." The word Paul chooses here does not mean "dead" in the typical sense. The Greek word used is apothnēskō, which means to die off, either literally or figuratively. This word can refer to literal death or the figurative death of a person, such as in the case of divorce. Let's explore other scriptures where Paul uses this word in a figurative sense.

Romans 6:8 (KJV)
Now if we be dead with Christ, we believe that we shall also live
with him:

Romans 7:9 (KJV)
For I was alive without the law once: but when the commandment
came, sin revived, and I died.

1 Corinthians 15:22 (KJV)
For as in Adam all die, even so in Christ shall all be made alive.

Colossians 3:3 (KJV)
For ye are dead, and your life is hid with Christ in God.

1 Corinthians 15:31 (KJV)
I protest by your rejoicing which I have in Christ Jesus our Lord,
I die daily.

In all of the above scriptures, Paul is describing a figurative death and not a literal death. Paul did not literally die daily. So, Paul's use of the word apothnēskō does not contradict the law of Moses. This word could be used for a husband who is deceased or divorced, both of which have brought the marriage to an end.

1 Corinthians 7:39 (Koimaō)

We have a similar problem with 1 Corinthians 7:39. Paul chose to use the word koimaō. This word means to put to sleep. It can be used to mean death or death metaphorically.

1 Corinthians 7:39 (KJV)
The wife is bound by the law as long as her husband liveth; but if
her husband be dead (koimaō), she is at liberty to be married to
whom she will; only in the Lord.

This is the same word Jesus used in John 11 to describe Lazarus. Notice the disciples' response—they did not think Lazarus was literally dead.

John 11:11-12 (KJV)

11. These things said he: and after that he saith unto them, Our friend Lazarus sleepeth (koimaō); but I go, that I may awake him out of sleep.

12. Then said his disciples, Lord, if he sleep, he shall do well.

The disciples' thought Jesus was saying that Lazarus was resting. Another example is Jesus found his disciples sleeping.

Luke 22:45 (KJV)
And when he rose up from prayer, and was come to his disciples, he found them sleeping (koimaō) for sorrow,

The problem is that people forget how we use the word "dead" all the time. For example: "I'm dead tired," "The town was dead after the factory closed down," "My phone is dead," or "After the scandal, his political career was dead."

So, once again, Paul's use of the word koimaō could mean a husband who is literally dead or one who is metaphorically dead. A husband who is metaphorically dead means that his role as a husband has come to an end.

1 CORINTHIANS CHAPTER 7

To understand this chapter, it is essential to understand the book of Corinthians as a whole. The entire book is a series of corrections. Paul addressed several issues the church was facing, such as division among members, dishonor and irreverence in communion, disorder when prophesying, and many other concerns.

Paul begins chapter 7 by answering a question that had been asked of him: "Is it good for a man not to touch a woman?"

The church in Corinth had begun practicing celibacy, believing it would elevate their spirituality. As a result, single people refused to marry, those who were betrothed broke off their engagements, and some married couples separated or even divorced. However, this practice led to problems with immorality within the church.

> 1 Corinthians 7:1 (International Standard Version)
> 1. Now about what you asked: "Is it advisable for a man not to touch a woman inappropriately?"
> 2. Yes, and yet because sexual immorality is so rampant, every man should have his own wife, and every woman should have her own husband.

To address the rampant sexual immorality, Paul instructed wives to have sex with their "own" husbands and husbands to have sex with their "own" wives. He also advised those who were not married to get married. Paul went so far as to state in verse five that even when praying and fasting, spouses should not abstain from sex unless mutually agreed upon. Paul warned that abstinence in marriage opens a door for Satan to cause temptation due to "incontinency".

Throughout the chapter, Paul emphasizes how one can serve God better while single. However, if someone struggles with celibacy, they should marry, and marriage is not a sin.

Paul mentions six marital statuses in this chapter: (1) believers married to believers, (2) believers married to unbelievers, (3) the unmarried, (4) widows, (5) virgins, and (6) betrothed.

Many teach that the "unmarried" refers to those who are single. However, this is not accurate. The unmarried group actually refers to those who are divorced, not those who are single. Those who are single are referred to as virgins in this context. Paul specifically distinguishes the widows from the unmarried. The Hebrew word "agamos" is used to describe a woman who has "departed" from her husband, meaning a divorced woman, not simply someone who is separated. "Agamos" refers to a woman who was previously married but is now unmarried.

1 Corinthians 7:11 (KJV)
But and *if she depart, let her remain unmarried (agamos)*, or be reconciled to [her] husband: and let not the husband put away [his] wife.

Christians often use 1 Corinthians 7:11 to argue that reconciliation with a spouse is the only option and that remarriage is only permissible once the spouse dies. This interpretation is incorrect. Notice that Paul instructs a married woman, and not a single woman in this verse, to remain "unmarried" (agamos). He is addressing couples who have already divorced and urging them to return to each other, as they were in error for embracing the doctrine of celibacy.

In verse eight, Paul distinguishes between the unmarried and the widows. He specifically tells the unmarried (agamos) to get married.

1 Corinthians 7:8-9 (KJV)
8. I say therefore to the unmarried (agamos) and widows, It is good for them if they abide even as I.
9. But if they cannot contain, let them marry: for it is better to marry than to burn.

Paul instructed both the divorced and the widowed to marry, stating it is better to "marry than to burn."

In his conclusion, Paul says that if a man is married, he should not seek a divorce. If he is divorced, he should not be eager to remarry. However, if he does remarry, "it is not a sin." Likewise, if a virgin marries, it is also not a sin.

1 Corinthians 7:27-28 (KJV)
27. Art thou bound unto a wife? seek not to be loosed. Art thou loosed from a wife? seek not a wife.
28. But and if thou marry, thou hast not sinned; and if a virgin marry, she hath not sinned. Nevertheless such shall have trouble in the flesh: but I spare you.

God Blesses Remarriage

I've heard some Christians say that God would never bless a second marriage unless a spouse has died. They often point to examples like Abraham marrying Keturah after Sarah's death, or Ruth marrying Boaz after becoming a widow. Boaz, the great-grandfather of David, is frequently mentioned in Christian teachings on marriage as their union is seen as divinely orchestrated.

But is there an example in Scripture of a second marriage following a divorce? Surprisingly, the answer is yes.

Exodus 2:1-2 (KJV)
1. And there went a man of the house of Levi, and took [to wife] a
daughter of Levi.
2. And the woman conceived, and bare a son: and when she saw
him that he [was a] goodly [child], she hid him three months.

Exodus chapter 2 describes the marriage of Moses' parents, Amram and Jochebed. What many may not realize is that this was actually their remarriage. Moses was the youngest of three siblings—Aaron and Miriam were born during Amram and Jochebed's first marriage. After Pharaoh issued the decree to kill all Hebrew male infants, Amram divorced Jochebed to avoid bringing more children into such danger.

According to rabbinic tradition, Miriam prophesied that her mother would give birth to a son who would deliver Israel from Egyptian bondage. This prophecy prompted Amram to remarry Jochebed. Therefore, the marriage mentioned in Exodus 2 was their second union.

Some might argue that this was merely a reconciliation, not a remarriage. However, there's more to the story. Moses, Aaron, and Miriam had two half-brothers—Eldad and Medad. These two were sons of Jochebed from her marriage to Elizaphan, whose name is recorded in Numbers 34:25.

Numbers 34:25 (KJV)
And the prince of the tribe of the children of Zebulun, Elizaphan
the son of Parnach.

One version of the story holds that Jochebed married Elizaphan after her divorce from Amram, and later remarried Amram. This account supports the idea of remarriage after divorce within the biblical narrative. However, there is another interpretation.

The renowned biblical commentator Rosh (Rabbenu Asher ben Jehiel) also agrees that Eldad and Medad were half-brothers to Moses, but he presents a different view—arguing that they shared a father, not a mother.

Following the Exodus from Egypt, Moses appointed seventy elders to help judge the nation of Israel, forming what would eventually become the Sanhedrin. Eldad and Medad were among those chosen. Notably, they were the two men who remained outside the camp, yet the Spirit of God rested upon them, and they began to prophesy—demonstrating their divine selection and unique role in Israel's history.

Numbers 11:26-27 (KJV)
26. But there remained two [of the] men in the camp, the name of the one [was] Eldad, and the name of the other Medad: and the spirit rested upon them; and they [were] of them that were written, but went not out unto the tabernacle: and they prophesied in the camp.
27. And there ran a young man, and told Moses, and said, Eldad and Medad do prophesy in the camp.

According to rabbinical teachings, Eldad and Medad prophesied about a future war with Gog and Magog, declaring that the Messiah would be involved. These prophecies are not recorded in the Bible. However, the prophet Ezekiel also prophesied against Gog in chapters 38 and 39, describing how God would fight alongside Israel. In that battle, God promised to send pestilence, rainstorms, hailstones, fire, and brimstone. These five divine elements signified that God—specifically, the Messiah—would join in the fight, just as Eldad and Medad had foretold.

In Numbers 11:25, when the seventy elders began to prophesy, the spirit of prophecy rested on them only temporarily. However, the Midrash states that, unlike the others, the prophecy of Eldad and Medad was permanent and came directly from God Himself.

What became of them? Eldad and Medad were the only two elders from the seventy who entered the Promised Land under Joshua's leadership. They outlived their half-siblings—Miriam, Aaron, and Moses—and were blessed by God with long life.

God blessed the second marriage of Amram and Jochebed with the birth of Moses. And He blessed Eldad and Medad, the half-brothers, with divine favor and longevity. Stories like these are rarely taught in church. Many often portray God as angry, vengeful, and merciless in the Old Testament, but loving and merciful in the New Testament. Yet God is the same—He does not change.

Malachi 3:6 (KJV)
"For I am the LORD, I change not..."

Even the prophet Jonah, in his anger, admitted that he knew God would show mercy to Nineveh. That's why he initially refused to go. Jonah wanted God to destroy the city. Nineveh, a major city in Assyria, belonged to the nation that had conquered the northern kingdom of Israel—killing many and exiling the rest. So, for God to send an Israelite prophet to warn their enemies was unthinkable to Jonah. Yet, in Jonah's own words, we see a clear picture of God's consistent character.

Jonah 4:2 (KJV)
"And he prayed unto the LORD, and said, I pray thee, O LORD, [was] not this my saying, when I was yet in my country? Therefore I fled before unto Tarshish: for I knew that *thou [art] a gracious God, and merciful, slow to anger, and of great kindness, and repentest thee of the evil.*"

The Old Testament God was a gracious God, merciful, slow to anger, and of great kindness. God never changed. He is the same yesterday, today, and forever.

Psalm 103:8 (KJV)
The LORD [is] merciful and gracious, slow to anger, and plenteous in mercy.

Psalm 145:8 (KJV)
The LORD [is] gracious, and full of compassion; slow to anger, and of great mercy.

Why So Many Widows?

While reading the New Testament, a particular detail began to stand out. In Acts chapter six, we find the Grecian Christians disputing with the Hebrew Christians over the daily distribution of food to the widows in Jerusalem. This issue prompted the twelve apostles to appoint seven deacons to manage the matter.

Later, in 1 Corinthians 7, Paul tells the widows in Corinth to marry, stating it is "better to marry than to burn." In his letter to Timothy, Paul presents a more detailed strategy for addressing the large number of widows in Ephesus. He instructs Timothy that the church is only responsible for caring for a "widow indeed," and he outlines specific qualifications for this designation. He tells Timothy to urge the children, nephews (1 Timothy 5:4), and believing women (1 Timothy 5:16) to care for their widowed relatives, thereby relieving the church of that responsibility. Paul further instructs that widows under sixty years old should not be included in the official list and that young widows should remarry and bear children.

One overlooked detail in all of this is Paul's repeated encouragement for widows to remarry. This tends to be missed because, in the modern church, remarriage is often seen as permissible for widows but forbidden for divorced women.

However, in Judaism, both widows and divorcees are encouraged to remarry based on God's declaration in Genesis 2:18: "It is not good that the man should be alone." Interestingly, Judaism takes a view opposite to that of many Christian denominations. Rabbi Maurice Lamm, in his book The Jewish Way in Love and Marriage, explains in his article "Remarriage" on Chabad.org: "Just as divorce frees her to marry, so does death." In Jewish culture, remarriage after divorce or widowhood is expected, not discouraged. This directly contradicts the modern church's popular teaching that only death ends a marriage.

If remarriage after widowhood was so culturally accepted, why then was Paul constantly encouraging widows to marry? Why were there so many widows in the early church? If it was not considered sinful, why did Paul emphasize it so strongly?

Another intriguing detail is Paul's use of the phrase "the wife of one man" as a qualification for a widow indeed (1 Timothy 5:9). This phrase is unique in scripture. Curious about its origin, I searched Jewish traditions but found no equivalent. However, turning to Roman culture, I discovered the answer.

The term univira in Roman society referred to a "one-husband woman." Latin-dictionary.net defines univira as a woman married only once. Roman society idealized the univira—typically a woman who married as a virgin and either predeceased her husband or never remarried, even after divorce. In time, the term also came to include divorced women who chose not to remarry.

This ideal was modeled after a Roman woman named Livia Drusilla. According to Encyclopedia Britannica, Livia, the daughter of a Roman senator, was a politician and the wife of Caesar Augustus. Born January 30, 58 BC, and dying in 29 AD, she was known for her loyalty, dignity, intelligence, and influence. She had two sons from her first marriage—Tiberius and Drusus—before divorcing her husband to marry Augustus. Though she and Augustus had no children together, her son Tiberius would eventually become emperor.

Roman historian Tacitus portrayed Livia in a negative light, accusing her of manipulating her way into political power and calling her a "blight." Despite this, Encyclopedia.com notes that Livia became "a revered model of correct feminine behavior" for generations. She was admired for being austere, conservative, faithful, and intelligent. She was skilled in diplomacy and was the owner of several business ventures. After Augustus's death, Livia never remarried. She was adopted into the Julian family, renamed Julia Augusta, and became a priestess in the cult of Augustus. In 42 AD, her grandson, Emperor Claudius, officially deified her. Her image appeared on coins, statues, and artwork, and she remained a symbol of Roman feminine virtue. However, her popularity also led to a decline in birth rates, as many Roman women sought to emulate her by remaining univira. The empire later had to create laws encouraging remarriage to reverse this trend.

Understanding Livia's influence is crucial. Paul, born around 5 AD, would have been about 24 years of age when Livia died in 29 AD. The First Letter to Timothy is believed to have been written around 55 AD, and Paul was martyred around 64 AD. This means Paul was well aware of who Livia was and the social standards she represented in Roman culture.

Although Paul borrowed the univira concept when describing the qualifications for a widow indeed, he still strongly encouraged widows to remarry. In his letter to Timothy, he tells the young widows in Ephesus to marry and bear children. In Paul's time, remarriage for widows in Rome was viewed as socially undesirable—unfashionable even. But Paul saw how some widows had become idle, gossipy, and busybodies. To protect them from becoming entangled in behavior that would pull them away from the faith, Paul encouraged remarriage.

Despite modern teachings that suggest remarriage after divorce is sinful while remarriage after widowhood is not, Paul's letters show a more nuanced and culturally aware approach. His guidance was shaped not only by spiritual insight but also by the social norms and pressures of his time.

1 Timothy 5:14-15 (NLT)

14. So I advise these younger widows to marry again, have children, and take care of their own homes. Then the enemy will not be able to say anything against them.

15. For I am afraid that some of them have already gone astray and now follow Satan.

WHERE CURRENT TEACHINGS ON DIVORCE COME FROM

There are several popular teachings on divorce within the church. These include beliefs such as: a divorced person cannot remarry or else their second marriage is considered adultery; a woman cannot divorce her husband; adultery is the only valid reason for divorce; and that God only recognizes a person's first marriage. Though these teachings often use scripture for support, they begin to unravel when the full context of scripture is considered.

The current teachings on divorce and remarriage in the church have evolved over time. Interestingly, they did not originate with Jesus, the apostles, or the early church fathers. It wasn't until about 100 years after the birth of the church that new views on adultery, divorce, and remarriage began to emerge.

One such example is The Shepherd of Hermas, a Christian literary work written in the 2nd century. There are varying opinions on who Hermas was. It is believed that the author was the brother of Pius, Bishop of Rome (around 140–154 AD), though the true identity remains uncertain.

The book contains five visions experienced by the author. In these visions, he receives twelve mandates (moral commandments) and ten similitudes (parables) from a figure known as "the Shepherd," who calls himself a minister of repentance. The Shepherd appears to the author during prayer, clothed in a white cloak, carrying a bag and staff.

In Command Four, we find a conversation between the author and the Shepherd concerning an unfaithful wife:

Command IV

4. And I said unto him, "Sir, suffer me to speak a little to you." He bade me say on. And I answered, "Sir, if a man that is faithful in the Lord has a wife and discovers her in adultery, does he sin if he continues to live with her?"

5. And he said unto me, "As long as he is ignorant of her sin, he commits no fault in living with her. But if a man knows his wife has offended, and she does not repent but continues in her fornication, and he still remains with her, he becomes guilty of her sin and partakes in her adultery."

6. And I said unto him, "What, then, should be done if the woman continues in her sin?" He answered, "Let her husband put her away and remain by himself. But if he puts her away and marries another, he also commits adultery."

7. And I said, "What if the woman who is put away repents and desires to return to her husband? Should she be received by him?" He said unto me, "Yes; and if her husband refuses to receive her, he sins and commits a great offense against himself. For he ought to receive the offender if she repents—but not repeatedly."

8. "For the servants of God, there is only one repentance. For this reason, a man who puts away his wife should not marry another, because she may repent."

9. "This applies equally to both the man and the woman. They commit adultery not only by polluting the flesh but also by forming an image. If a woman persists in such behavior and does not repent, depart from her and live not with her; otherwise, you also shall partake in her sin."

10. "Therefore, it is commanded that both the man and the woman remain unmarried, because such persons may yet repent."

This passage teaches that if a man or woman is unaware of their spouse's unfaithfulness, they are not guilty of sin. However, once they become aware of the adultery and the offending spouse refuses to repent, remaining in the marriage makes them a participant in that sin.

This raises an important question: Does this concept align with scripture? Is a person guilty of adultery simply because their spouse committed adultery?

The answer is no. This concept does not align with the scriptures. As Paul stated in Galatians 1:8, "But though we, or an angel from heaven, preach any other gospel unto you than that which we have preached unto you, let him be accursed." This idea is not consistent with the gospel that was preached by the apostles.

In Numbers 5, Moses outlines a specific procedure for the priest to follow when a woman is accused of infidelity. Notably, verse 31 states that the husband does not bear the iniquity of his wife. By the same standard, a wife does not bear the iniquity of her husband. Each person is responsible for their own sin, and guilt is not transferable simply by remaining in a marriage.

Numbers 5:31 (KJV)
Then shall the man be guiltless from iniquity, and this woman shall bear her iniquity.

Numbers 5:31 (NLT)
The husband will be innocent of any guilt in this matter, but his wife will be held accountable for her sin."

Let's say a person is guilty of the crime of adultery, and this means their spouse is also guilty. Shouldn't this apply to other crimes or sins as well? Or is this concept limited only to adultery? We do not find this to be the case in several examples in the Bible.

In the story of Ananias and Sapphira, the couple lied to the church regarding the sale of a piece of property. Sapphira was complicit in Ananias' plan. They agreed to deceive Apostle Peter.

Acts 5:1-2 (KJV)
1. But a certain man named Ananias, with Sapphira his wife, sold a possession,
2. And kept back part of the price, his wife also being privy to it, and brought a certain part, and laid it at the apostles' feet.

In this case, the couple was in agreement, and they both suffered the consequences. However, in the story of Nabal and Abigail, Nabal was a churlish, evil man, but Abigail had a beautiful countenance. Abigail did not suffer the same fate as her husband. God does not view husbands or wives as partakers in their spouse's sin.

In verse six, the Shepherd said to the author that if the woman decides not to end her affair, the husband is required to "put her away." When he does, he cannot remarry because the second marriage would be adulterous. Does this align with the scriptures? No.

An adulterous marriage was not one following a divorce. An adulterous marriage was a marriage to another while the current marriage persisted.

In the story of Hosea, God did not require Hosea to put Gomer away. Hosea was aware of what Gomer was doing, but he was not guilty of adultery. God required Hosea to go after his wife, who "played the harlot."

In Jeremiah 3:8, the prophet calls Israel an unfaithful wife. Israel committed adultery against God. The act of adultery is called backsliding in this scripture.

Jeremiah 3:8 (KJV)
And I saw, when for all the causes whereby backsliding Israel committed adultery I had put her away, and given her a bill of divorce; yet her treacherous sister Judah feared not, but went and played the harlot also.

In this passage, Israel backslid. Because she refused to repent (her apostasy), God "put her away" and gave her a bill of divorce. These are the same steps outlined in the law of Moses, found in Deuteronomy 24:1. The law did not forbid them from remarrying following a divorce.

It is important that we understand why Hermas said that if you get divorced, you are to remain unmarried. He explained in verses seven through ten that the husband had to take the woman back if she ever repented. The man was to remain unmarried in case the woman decided to return. If he or she refused to take the other back, then that person had sinned, a sin of unforgiveness.

This idea also contradicts the scriptures. If the woman was simply "put away," she could not remarry because her marriage was considered valid by the court. She could not remarry unless she had a bill of divorce to present to the priest. However, once she received her bill of divorcement, she was free to marry another man. She was not required to return to the husband who had divorced her. Likewise, the husband was not required to take back a repented wife. Forgiveness and restoration are not the same. Though Adam received forgiveness for breaking covenant (Hosea 6:7 NLT) with God in the garden, he was not struck dead; instead, he was never allowed access to the garden again.

Deuteronomy 24:1-2 (KJV)
1. When a man hath taken a wife, and married her, and it come to pass that she find no favour in his eyes, because he hath found some uncleanness in her: then let him write her a bill of divorcement, and give [it] in her hand, and send her out of his house.
2. And when she is departed out of his house, she may go and be ***another man's [wife].***

Doctrine of Devils

Paul makes a very serious statement to Timothy. He explained that a doctrine of devils would eventually seep into the church—originating from seducing spirits—and warned Timothy not to listen to or embrace it. According to Paul, one clear mark of this doctrine would be the forbidding of marriage.

1 Timothy 4:1–3 (KJV)
1. Now the Spirit speaketh expressly, that in the latter times some shall depart from the faith, giving heed to seducing spirits, and doctrines of devils;
2. Speaking lies in hypocrisy; having their conscience seared with a hot iron;
3. Forbidding to marry, and commanding to abstain from meats, which God hath created to be received with thanksgiving of them which believe and know the truth.

Some have attempted to connect this doctrine to teachings within the Catholic Church. However, the Catholic Church does not forbid marriage; rather, they require their priests to voluntarily take a vow of celibacy. That is a choice, not a prohibition.

Interestingly, the words "remarriage," "divorcee," or "divorced" do not appear in Scripture. These terms are modern cultural constructs. However, it is clear that any forbidding of marriage—especially for those previously married—should be regarded as a doctrine of devils, as Paul warned.

The Law of Moses did not forbid marriage to those who were divorced or widowed in the Old Testament, and neither did the early church. In fact, the Jewish community expected a divorced or widowed person to remarry. This was also the cultural norm among the Gentiles in Rome.

Unfortunately, as Paul predicted, this deceptive doctrine has become increasingly prevalent within the church today—especially in the form of prohibiting remarriage for those who are divorced.

WE ARE NOT UNDER THE LAW

Realizing that Jesus was addressing the unethical practice of annulling a divorce without informing the other party—leading to countless women unknowingly entering into adulterous marriages—raises a major question. Where does this leave us as the church? If Jesus was not teaching against the law of Moses, then what is the correct position regarding divorce?

First, we must understand the law of Moses in its proper context. The law of Moses imposed certain legal requirements on its citizens. For example, every woman was required to have a dowry, and every woman had to have a marriage contract with an agreed-upon amount designated in case of divorce or the husband's death, which would be enforced by the court. The woman could not initiate the divorce through the court; it was required to be done by the man. Children born of adulterous unions were ostracized. Priests were forbidden from marrying certain women based on their status. A woman could not be divorced from her husband, marry another man, and then return to her first husband. Additionally, if a man or woman was accused of adultery or infidelity, they were forbidden from marrying the person they were suspected of cheating with, forever. Such laws do not exist in our society today.

While many view the law of Moses as "the word of God" (and rightly so), we rarely view it as the set of laws specifically governing the nation of Israel. These laws applied only to their citizens. Those who joined the nation became Israelites and were required to follow the law of Moses (Numbers 15:29), just like any natural-born Hebrew (Jew). The law of

Moses was not a law imposed on other nations, though most nations have similar civil laws—such as those against murder, adultery, or theft. The penalties for such crimes differed from nation to nation.

Those who were born Jews were required to observe the religious laws of Moses, no matter where they resided. The priesthood of Zadok (2 Samuel, 1 Kings) is important because it established what the Israelites were to do if they were no longer living in Israel. When the nation of Israel found itself in exile, we see these instructions from Zadok being implemented. The religious practices mentioned in books like Daniel, Esther, Ezra, Nehemiah, and others show how these practices continued while Israel was in exile.

Another important point is that the law of Moses was also connected to Israel's covenant with God.

Psalm 78:10 (KJV)
They kept not the covenant of God, and refused to walk in his law.

The covenant between God and the nation of Israel required all Israelites and converts to keep the law in its entirety. It was one law made up of 613 commandments. Breaking one law was the same as breaking the entire law of Moses, as James explains.

James 2:10 (KJV)
For whosoever shall keep the whole law, and yet offend in one [point], he is guilty of all.

Galatians 5:3 (KJV)
For I testify again to every man that is circumcised, that he is a debtor to do the whole law.

This was the agreement made between God and Israel: they agreed to keep the entire law when Moses brought it to them as God's mediator.

Deuteronomy 28:15 (KJV) But it shall come to pass, if thou wilt not hearken unto the voice of the LORD thy God, to **observe to do all his** _**commandments**_ **and his** _**statutes**_ which I command thee this day; that all these curses shall come upon thee, and overtake thee:

Deuteronomy 27:26 (KJV) Cursed [be] he that confirmeth not [all] the words of this law to do them. ***And all the people shall say, Amen.***

In Deuteronomy 27:26, the people entered into a covenant with God. Their "amen" was their agreement to keep all the words of the law. They agreed to receive both the blessings of God and the curses if they transgressed the law at any point.

The major problem with the Christian viewpoint regarding the law of Moses is that we stress certain laws and ignore others. We pick which laws to keep and follow, as we see with the debate over keeping the Sabbath. People argue about which day the Sabbath is to be kept but ignore the 39 Melakhot, which are the 39 categories of prohibited activities on the Sabbath according to biblical law. Those under the law could not pick and choose which laws to keep or how those laws would be followed. The law was, and is, required to be kept in its entirety. Jesus was born under the law. This means He kept the law in its entirety and never transgressed it.

Galatians 4:4 (KJV)
But when the fulness of the time was come, God sent forth his
Son, made of a woman, ***made under the law***,

Jesus was made under the law. This means Jesus was born under the covenant God made with Israel through Moses (Torah). So, Jesus was required to live according to the law of Moses and not contrary to it, as many Christians suggest. Jesus was circumcised by a priest, fulfilling the law of Brit Milah—the Covenant of Circumcision (Luke 2:21). He also observed the Jewish festivals (mo'adim, or appointed times) such as the Feast of Unleavened Bread and the Feast of Tabernacles (John 7:10). Jesus kept the Sabbath which "was his custom" and would read Scriptures in the synagogue (Luke 4:16). Jesus wore the garments of a Torah-observant Jewish rabbi, which included the Tzitzit—the ritual fringes commanded in the Torah. In Matthew 9:20, the woman with the issue of blood touches "the hem of His garment." The Greek word translated as "hem" is (kraspedon), which specifically refers to the fringe, tassel, or border of a garment—clearly identifying the Tzitzit. As a Jewish Rabbi who observed the commandments of the Torah, Jesus would have worn either a Tallit Katan (a small four-cornered undergarment with Tzitzit) or a mantle with Tzitzit attached, in accordance with Numbers 15:37–40, where God commands the children of Israel to wear fringes on the corners of their garments to remember the commandments. Jesus kept the law in its entirety, not in part, which would have been necessary for Jesus to have been the blameless and sinless lamb of God.

Redemption is a concept we see throughout the law of Moses. To redeem means to ransom or purchase land. Through His blood (Revelation 5:9), Jesus redeemed those who were under the law from the curse of the law. Why were those who kept the law under a curse? The agreement made between Israel and God had many curses attached to it. So, Jesus became cursed so that He might redeem us from the curse.

Galatians 3:13 (KJV)
Christ hath redeemed us from the curse of the law, being made a
curse for us: for it is written, Cursed [is] every one that hangeth on
a tree:

With this being said, we are not under the law and are not required to live according to the law of Moses. The born-again believer is not under the law but under grace (Romans 6:14-15). To live by the law now would bring us back under the curses and would require us to keep the law in its entirety. Breaking even one law would cause the curses attached to that covenant to come upon us. All the curses are listed in Deuteronomy 27, beginning at verse 11, and in Deuteronomy 28, beginning at verse 15.

We Died to the Law

Paul also explained how those under the law were set free. It's not simply a decision to walk away from the Old Covenant and enter into the

New Covenant. Paul explained that we died to the law through the body of Jesus Christ. When Jesus died, we died with Him, freeing us from the first marriage to the law. Our death allows us to enter into a new covenant with Christ.

Romans 7:4 (NIV)
So, my brothers and sisters, **you also died to the law** through the body of Christ, that you might belong to another, to him who was raised from the dead, in order that we might bear fruit for God.

Romans 7:4 (KJV)
Wherefore, my brethren, **ye also are become dead to the law** by the body of Christ; that ye should be married to another, [even] to him who is raised from the dead, that we should bring forth fruit unto God.

Paul gave a very strong warning regarding those who teach we are to live according to the law of Moses and by faith. In Philippians, Paul warned against those who were pushing circumcision as a requirement for salvation. Though circumcision is a requirement to live in compliance with the law of Moses, it is not a requirement to be saved. (And please do not confuse the medical practice of circumcision with brit milah — "the covenant of circumcision" — required by the law of Moses.)

Philippians 3:2 (NLT) says,
"Watch out for those dogs, those people who do evil, those mutilators who say you must be circumcised to be saved."

We are Saved by Faith and Not by Works

Paul also addressed this issue in Galatians, where a group called the Judaizers came into the church, teaching the early Christians to live by faith and according to the law of Moses. Paul explained that Believers were not justified (made righteous before God) by the law. Righteousness comes by faith and faith alone. The Israelites were required to keep the law just as any citizen in any country is expected to follow the (federal) laws of their country. But keeping the law did not make them righteous — no more than us being law-abiding citizens would make us righteous in God's eyes.

Galatians 3:10-13 (KJV)

10. For as many as are of the works of the law are under the curse: for it is written, Cursed [is] every one that continueth not in all things which are written in the book of the law to do them.

11. But that **no man is justified by the law in the sight of God**, [it is] evident: for, The just shall live by faith.

12. And **the law is not of faith**: but, The man that doeth them shall live in them.

13. Christ hath redeemed us from the curse of the law, being made a curse for us: for it is written, Cursed [is] every pone that hangeth on a tree:

Galatians 3:10-13 (NLT)

10. But those who depend on the law to make them right with God are under his curse, for the Scriptures say, "Cursed is everyone who does not observe and obey **all the commands** that are written in God's Book of the Law."

11. So it is clear that **no one can be made right with God by trying to keep the law**. For the Scriptures say, "It is through faith that a righteous person has life."

12. This way of faith is very different from the way of law, which says, "It is through obeying the law that a person has life."

13. But Christ has rescued us from the curse pronounced by the law. When he was hung on the cross, he took upon himself the curse for our wrongdoing. For it is written in the Scriptures, "Cursed is everyone who is hung on a tree."

The law is holy (Romans 7:12), but it was never designed to make men righteous. Otherwise, we would be made righteous by works—by our own will and human efforts. Righteousness does not come through works; otherwise, we would be able to boast in our efforts, and those with the most money and resources would be considered the most righteous among us because they could do more for those in need. Feeding and clothing the homeless does not make us righteous—only faith does. And righteousness does not come through works in the context of keeping the law of Moses. We are saved through faith.

Ephesians 2:8-9 (KJV)
8. For by grace are ye saved through faith; and that not of yourselves: [it is] the gift of God:
9. *Not of works, lest any man* should boast.

There was no law that could give people life. If there had been, God would have given that commandment, and we could have been made righteous through the law.

Galatians 3:21 (KJV):
"Is the law then against the promises of God? God forbid: for if there had been a law given which could have given life, verily righteousness should have been by the law."

We are made righteous by faith, which was the same requirement found in the Old Testament before the law was given. Abraham believed God, and it was credited to him as righteousness (Genesis 15:6; Romans 4:3; Galatians 3:6; James 2:23).

Hebrews 11 highlights what is often called the "Hall of Faith," featuring individuals like Abel, Enoch, Noah, Abraham, Sarah, and others. These Old Testament saints were made righteous by faith because they believed God.

How did Jesus fulfill the Law and the Prophets? He brought them to completion. With the prophets, this is especially clear. Throughout His life, Jesus would make statements such as, "This was done so that the Scripture might be fulfilled," demonstrating how His actions and experiences brought prophetic words to pass.

Matthew 1:22 (KJV)
Now all this was done, that it might be fulfilled which was spoken
of the Lord by the prophet, saying,

According to Bible scholars, Jesus fulfilled between 300 and 570 Old Testament prophecies. For example, He was born into the tribe of Judah (Genesis 49:10; Isaiah 11:1) and born in Bethlehem (Micah 5:2), making it easier to recognize the fulfillment of prophecy.

Jesus also fulfilled the law. This does not mean He came to fix or correct it. The law had no flaws or errors. It was, and still is, perfect (Psalm 19:7). However, the law could not—and was never intended to—make people righteous.

1 Timothy 1:9 (KJV)
Knowing this, that the law is not made for a righteous man, but for
the lawless and disobedient, for the ungodly and for sinners, for
unholy and profane, for murderers of fathers and murderers of
mothers, for manslayers,

The law revealed sin. Paul explained he would not have known what sin was to God without the law.

Romans 7:7 (KJV)
What shall we say then? [Is] the law sin? God forbid. **Nay, I had
not known sin, but by the law**: for I had not known lust, except
the law had said, Thou shalt not covet.

However, the law—both civil and religious—only required human discipline. It demanded strong devotion but did not address a person's inward struggles, desires, or lusts.

Colossians 2:23 (NLT)
These rules may seem wise because they require strong devotion,
pious self-denial, and severe bodily discipline. But they provide no
help in conquering a person's evil desires.

What the law lacked by design was faith. Obeying the law did not require faith. Faith isn't needed to refrain from killing, bearing false witness, or keeping the Sabbath. Yet faith is the requirement for righteousness. "The just shall live by faith," as the Old Testament prophet Habakkuk explained:

Habakkuk 2:4 (KJV)
Behold, his soul which is lifted up is not upright in him: but the just shall live by his faith.

God established the system of faith in the Old Testament. Jesus brought the missing component to this system of righteousness: salvation through faith in His name. This is what brought the law and the prophets to their place of fulfillment. We are now saved through faith in Him—made righteous by confessing with our mouths that Jesus is Lord and believing in our hearts that He was raised on the third day.

Romans 10:9–10 (NLT)
9. If you openly declare that Jesus is Lord and believe in your heart that God raised him from the dead, you will be saved.
10. For it is by believing in your heart that you are made right with God, and it is by openly declaring your faith that you are saved.

The Law vs Grace

Does this mean that because Jesus fulfilled the law, we are now free to live however we choose? Absolutely not. Being under grace comes with a much greater responsibility than being under the law. Ask yourself: Which blood is holier—the blood of animals or the blood of Jesus?

Hebrews 10:26-29 (NLT)
26. Dear friends, if we deliberately continue sinning after we have received knowledge of the truth, there is no longer any sacrifice that will cover these sins.
27. There is only the terrible expectation of God's judgment and the raging fire that will consume his enemies.

28. For anyone who refused to obey the law of Moses was put to death without mercy on the testimony of two or three witnesses.

29. ***Just think how much worse the punishment will be for those who have trampled on the Son of God***, and have treated the blood of the covenant, which made us holy, as if it were common and unholy, and have insulted and disdained the Holy Spirit who brings God's mercy to us.

We Fulfill the Law by Keeping These Two Commandments

Though Jesus fulfilled the law, there is still a form of law-keeping required of us. Jesus explained that there are two commandments we must keep, and by doing so, we fulfill the entire Law of Moses—all 613 commandments.

Matthew 22:37-40 (KJV)
37. Jesus said unto him, Thou shalt love the Lord thy God with all thy heart, and with all thy soul, and with all thy mind.
38. This is the first and great commandment.
39. And the second [is] like unto it, Thou shalt love thy neighbour as thyself.
40. ***On these two commandments*** hang all the law and the prophets.

Galatians 5:14 (KJV)
For ***all the law is fulfilled in one word***, [even] in this; Thou shalt love thy neighbour as thyself.

Though many have mistakenly taught that Jesus introduced these as new laws for the New Testament Church, they are not new at all. Both commandments originate from the Law of Moses—Deuteronomy 6:5 and Leviticus 19:18. Jesus emphasized that these two commandments are the greatest because they summarize the entire Law of Moses.

Paul affirmed this by teaching that loving one another is the fulfillment of the law (Romans 13:8). He also explained that when we are led by the Spirit of God, we are no longer under the law (Galatians 5:18). This is the law that we, as New Testament believers, are called to live by. James referred to it as the royal law.

James 2:8-9 (NIV)

8. If you really keep the royal law found in Scripture, "Love your neighbor as yourself," you are doing right.

9. But if you show favoritism, you sin and are convicted by the law as lawbreakers.

A Different Priesthood

Another extremely critical doctrine that is often overlooked in Christianity is the priesthood we are under. The priesthood of Aaron required sacrifices, ceremonial washings, and strict adherence to the law. If we claim to be under the law, then we are obligated to keep it in its entirety, including all its priestly requirements. However, as Paul explained in Hebrews 9, we are now under a better covenant, one that was built upon the first but surpasses it in every way.

Hebrews 9:9-10 (NLT)

9 This is an illustration pointing to the present time. For the gifts and sacrifices that the priests offer are not able to cleanse the consciences of the people who bring them.

10 For that old system deals only with food and drink and various cleansing ceremonies--physical regulations that were in effect only until a better system could be established.

Understanding the old system is essential in order to fully understand Christ. However, we are no longer under the priesthood of Aaron; we are under the priesthood of Melchizedek.

Many Christians use Hebrews 7:12 to argue that Jesus changed the law of Moses:

Hebrews 7:12 (KJV)
"For the priesthood being changed, there is made of necessity a
change also of the law."

This verse does not say that God changed the law of Moses. Rather, it explains that God instituted a different law entirely—because the priesthood changed. Under the priesthood of Aaron, only men from the tribe of Levi could serve as priests, and only those from the house of Kohath could perform specific duties (Numbers 4:4). This law disqualified Jesus, who was born from the tribe of Judah.

Hebrews 7:14 (NLT)
"What I mean is, our Lord came from the tribe of Judah, and
Moses never mentioned priests coming from that tribe."

This presented a challenge, because Jesus had to come from the tribe of Judah, as prophesied by Jacob in Genesis 49:10. This tribal lineage gave Jesus the right to be King—the Lion of the tribe of Judah—but disqualified Him from serving as a high priest under the Levitical system.

Yet, Jesus was still made a high priest. Not by altering the law of Moses to accommodate Him, but by introducing a completely different priesthood—one based not on genealogy, but on an oath.

Hebrews 7:20–21 (NLT)
"This new system was established with a solemn oath. Aaron's
descendants became priests without such an oath."

This change in priesthood opened the door for believers to become both kings and priests—a royal priesthood (1 Peter 2:9). This was God's intention from the beginning: to establish a nation of priests (Exodus 19:6). However, this was not possible under the law of Moses.

Therefore, there was no alteration to the Law of Moses or to the Levitical priesthood. God did not change the law to allow priests from other tribes. Instead, He established a new priesthood—the order of Melchizedek—which is the priesthood under which the Church now operates. As Paul clearly stated in Hebrews 7:12, it was the priesthood that changed, not the Law of Moses.

Hebrews 7:12 (KJV)
For *the priesthood being changed*, there is made of necessity a change also of the law.

The conclusion is that the law of Moses does not apply to the Church. However, the law remains relevant to us as it serves as an example, a type, a shadow, and a schoolmaster that helps us understand spiritual truths.

Colossians 2:17 (NLT)
"For these rules are only shadows of the reality yet to come. And Christ himself is that reality."

The curse of the law has been done away with, but the blessings are not ours through the law; they are ours through the promises made to Abraham. Paul explained that the promises were made to Abraham, but the law was not given for another 430 years. The law did not nullify or void the promises. The promise and the law ran alongside each other until the birth of Jesus.

Our inheritance as saints of God is not tied to the law; it is tied to the promise.

Galatians 3:17-18 (NLT)
17. This is what I am trying to say: The agreement God made with Abraham could not be canceled 430 years later when God gave the law to Moses. God would be breaking his promise.
18. For if the inheritance could be received by keeping the law, then it would not be the result of accepting God's promise. But God graciously gave it to Abraham as a promise.

The promise child God promised to Abraham was not the child Isaac, it was Jesus. Paul explains this revelation in Galatians 3:16.

Galatians 3:16 (NLT)
God gave the promises to Abraham and his child. And notice that
the Scripture doesn't say "to his children," as if it meant many
descendants. Rather, it says "to his child"--and that, of course,
means Christ.

The promise made to Abraham was Jesus. This is how all the families of the earth would be blessed through Abraham. The inheritance promised to all who receive Christ is the Spirit of God, the Holy Spirit.

Galatians 3:14 (KJV)
That the blessing of Abraham might come on the Gentiles
through Jesus Christ; *that we might receive the promise of the
Spirit* through faith.

So, how are we to make sense of all of this in relation to divorce? We approach it in the same way we approach marriage. We do not follow the law of Moses when it comes to marriage. Christians do not use a ketubah or marriage agreements outlining the duties, responsibilities, and financial obligations of the husband. Christ has already done that for His bride (the Church), but Christians do not follow such a system for marriage. Interestingly, Christians follow Roman culture when it comes to marriage, rather than the Jewish system, and we follow a twisted version of Christ's teachings when it comes to divorce. In both cases, the Church is not following the Old Testament system, nor that which was established before the law was given.

Are we to follow the Jewish system of marriage or divorce? No, and doing so would require us to keep the entire law, all 613 commandments. We are no longer under the law. This is because Jesus fulfilled His assignment on the cross and also because of our obedience to the Spirit of God (Galatians 5:18).

WHEN DIVORCE BECAME NECESSARY

Jesus made some very significant statements regarding divorce that are relevant and important to the church.

Matthew 19:8 (KJV)
He saith unto them, Moses because of the hardness of your hearts suffered you to put away your wives: but from the beginning it was not so.

Mark 10:5 (KJV)
And Jesus answered and said unto them, For the hardness of your heart he wrote you this precept.

There are three statements of truth made by Jesus in these verses. Moses permitted men to put away their wives because of the hardness of men's hearts. The putting away of wives is a precept. And from the beginning, it was not so. Let's begin with "in the beginning."

From the Beginning, It Was Not So

The statement "from the beginning" refers to Adam and Eve. They serve as the example of God's original plan for marriage. However, we know that sin changed many things. God's curse upon Eve, following her disobedience by eating from the tree of the knowledge of good and evil, was that she would experience pain in childbirth and be ruled by her husband.

Genesis 3:16 (ESV)
To the woman he said, "I will surely multiply your pain in
childbearing; in pain you shall bring forth children. Your desire
shall be contrary to your husband, but he shall rule over you."

God's statement implies that this was not His original plan for women but how things would unfold from that point forward. Are women still experiencing pain during childbirth? Yes. God's plan and desire were altered by sin. God desires many things; however, sin and free will produce outcomes and consequences that are contrary to His desire. Is it God's desire that any should perish and go to hell? Absolutely not. And yet, hell is enlarging her mouth daily as souls go there to remain for eternity.

2 Peter 3:9 (CSB)
The Lord does not delay his promise, as some understand delay,
but is patient with you, *not wanting any to perish but all to
come to repentance*.

Isaiah 5:14 (KJV)
Therefore *hell hath enlarged herself, and opened her mouth
without measure*: and their glory, and their multitude, and their
pomp, and he that rejoiceth, shall descend into it.

God's intention was for the earth and all life on it to never experience death. Adam and Eve were created to be immortal and free from the effects of sin and death. However, sin corrupted man and all life on earth. Death, which entered this world through sin (Romans 5:12), has affected the entire planet, not just human beings but animals and plants alike. We hold on to the promise as part of our doctrine of faith that one day, death will be swallowed up.

1 Corinthians 15:54 (KJV)
So when this corruptible shall have put on incorruption, and this
mortal shall have put on immortality, then shall be brought to pass
the saying that is written, "Death is swallowed up in victory."

The effects of sin changed the DNA of man. Adam was made in God's image. He and Eve were perfect when God created them. They had no darkness in them. Mindsets and thoughts that are normal for us would have been foreign to them. Thoughts of selfishness, fear, anger, wrath, sadness, shame, anxiety, depression, despair, tiredness, condemnation, confusion, guilt, sorrow, and more would have been abnormal to their existence.

Genesis 2:25 says they were both naked and unashamed. But as soon as they ate the fruit, their "eyes were opened." They immediately hid, and for the first time, they felt fear. When questioned, they shifted blame and refused to take accountability. They were no longer immortal; they became mortal. They were no longer incorruptible; they became corruptible. Death and decay immediately began to affect not only their bodies but the entire world.

Concepts like repentance, forgiveness, redemption, grace, mercy, restoration, reconciliation, healing, resurrection, and more became necessities that man now required. God had to establish a new system of approaching Him, which now required the blood of animals. In Genesis 4, Cain and Abel brought sacrifices to God, a system that was not required "in the beginning."

Sin had an adverse effect on the hearts of people. The knowledge of good and evil awakened the dark side of man's consciousness. When Adam and Eve sinned, they immediately experienced a flood of emotions they had never encountered before: fear, shame, embarrassment, and more. They began lying and blame-shifting. Since that moment, man became dishonest, untrustworthy, jealous, angry, judgmental, self-absorbed, selfish, self-conscious, contradictory, envious, and exhibited many other qualities that cause covenants to fail.

God's intent was for man to be in communion and covenant with Him. God established this in the garden with Adam and Eve, as He would come in the cool of the day. Adam broke that covenant.

Hosea 6:7 (NLT)
But like Adam, you broke my covenant and betrayed my trust.

In addition, men have entered into covenants and agreements with evil spirits. In a world governed by sin, where there are covenants, divorce must also be an option. If people are unable to break a covenant, they would be bound to it, in agreement with evil spirits forever, with no way to be set free. Christians often say they can be set free "by the blood of Jesus," but fail to realize that the blood of Jesus is connected to covenant. Jesus explained that His blood was the blood of the New Testament (diathēkē). Diathēkē means covenant or compact.

2 Corinthians 6:14-17 (KJV)
14. Be ye not unequally *yoked* together with unbelievers: for what *fellowship* hath righteousness with unrighteousness? and what *communion* hath light with darkness?
15. And what *concord* hath Christ with Belial? or what *part* hath he that believeth with an infidel?
16. And what *agreement* hath the temple of God with idols? for ye are the temple of the living God; as God hath said, I will dwell in them, and walk in [them]; and I will be their God, and they shall be my people.
17. Wherefore come out from among them, and be ye separate, saith the Lord, and touch not the unclean [thing]; and I will receive you,

In the above passage, Paul uses many words associated with covenant: yoked, fellowship, concord, part, and agreement. Once a person or people group has been yoked, they are in communion, a concord has been established, and an agreement has been made. It is not simple to "come from among" and be "separate." A divorce is now required. These spiritual unions must be severed, and the oath or vow taken must be repudiated.

The Hebrew word for "bill of divorcement" is kᵊrîṯûṯ, which means divorce, dismissal, or divorcement. It comes from the root word kārat, which means: to cut, cut off, cut down, cut off a body part, cut out, eliminate, kill, or cut a covenant. As many debate whether God divorced Israel and Judah or only threatened to divorce them, the word kārat is used over 288 times in the scriptures. Those who broke covenant with God were cut off.

Exodus 31:14 (KJV)
Ye shall keep the sabbath therefore; for it [is] holy unto you: every one that defileth it shall surely be put to death: for whosoever doeth [any] work therein, that soul shall be ***cut off*** (kārat) from among his people.

Numbers 15:31 (KJV)
Because he hath despised the word of the LORD, and hath broken his commandment, that soul shall utterly be ***cut off*** (kārat); his iniquity [shall be] upon him.

Leviticus 18:29 (KJV)
For whosoever shall commit any of these abominations, even the souls that commit [them] shall be ***cut off*** (kārat) from among their people.

Numbers 15:31 (KJV)
Because he hath despised the word of the LORD, and hath broken his commandment, that soul shall utterly be ***cut off*** (kārat); his iniquity [shall be] upon him.

When an agreement or covenant is broken, the end result is the death of the agreement. There is a cutting off, or kārat, that occurs. Whatever was to be received through the agreement is now cut off. God promised Israel that He would bless them, sending rain and other resources. However, when they transgressed—often—they were cut off. In many cases, many people died, and others found themselves in bondage. There were four types of judgment: wild beasts, famine, pestilence, and the sword (war).

Ezekiel 14:21 (KJV)
For thus saith the Lord GOD; How much more when I send my
four sore judgments upon Jerusalem, the *sword*, and the
famine, and the noisome *beast*, and the *pestilence*, to cut off
from it man and beast?

Then God would raise up a prophet, judge, or scribe to send to the people, telling them to repent and what God would promise them if they returned to Him.

Sadly, covenants are made and broken because we live in a world where people do not keep or honor their word. This can apply to a vow of marriage between a couple or even a vow made to God.

Judicial Oaths

It is commonly taught that Jesus said we shouldn't swear or take an oath. However, this is another inaccurate teaching that is often taken out of context.

Matthew 5:34 (KJV)
But I say unto you, Swear not at all; neither by heaven; for it is
God's throne:

People ignore Jesus' first statement.

Matthew 5:33 (KJV)
Again, ye have heard that it hath been said by them of old time,
Thou shalt not *forswear* thyself, but shalt perform unto the Lord
thine oaths:

Jesus first quoted the law of Moses in verse 33. He was not contradicting the law of Moses in verse 34, which requires a man who has given an oath to keep it (Numbers 30:2). In verse 33, Jesus used the word "forswear," which means to perjure oneself. Jesus was referring to the law that required people to tell the truth under oath in court.

The Hebrew terms for "oath," alah and shebu'ah, are used interchangeably in the Old Testament. According to Jewishencyclopedia.com by the Executive Committee of the Editorial Board and Julius Rappoport, it explains that the "judicial oath was employed in civil cases only, never in criminal cases." The oath would be used in litigations concerning private property, but never in cases involving sacerdotal (priestly or religious) property. The oath was also used for movable property (assets that can be moved from one place to another), but not immovable property (property that cannot be moved, such as land or buildings).

Most importantly, an oath was required only when there was a lack of sufficient evidence on either side of a case. If neither party could present enough compelling evidence to support their claims, an oath would be administered as a way to secure a truthful declaration.

Exodus 22:10-11 (KJV)
10. If a man deliver unto his neighbour an ass, or an ox, or a sheep, or any beast, to keep; and it die, or be hurt, or driven away, no man seeing it:
11. Then shall an oath of the Lord be between them both, that he hath not put his hand unto his neighbour's goods; and the owner of it shall accept thereof, and he shall not make it good.

The oath wasn't required when there was adequate evidence, proper documentation, or a witness. The Biblical oath was imposed only upon the defendant. If the defendant committed perjury, they were not liable to the court, but to God Himself.

Jesus didn't contradict the law of Moses by saying people should commit perjury. Instead, He said if people give their word, they should keep it. In doing so, they won't have to forswear or commit perjury when brought before the judges (Beit Din) for not keeping their word or for breach of contract. Jesus explained, "Let your 'yes' mean 'yes,' and your 'no' mean 'no.'"

Matthew 5:37 (KJV)
But let your communication be, Yea, yea; Nay, nay: for whatsoever
is more than these cometh of evil.

In other words, Jesus said to be honest and maintain integrity. However, most people do not live with integrity. They break their word, their promises, and their covenants. Jesus advised that to avoid being brought to court and committing perjury (forswearing), one should simply keep their word. It's better not to make a vow than to make one and fail to fulfill it. This is a principle that can be found in the Old Testament.

Ecclesiastes 5:4-5 (KJV)
4. When thou vowest a vow unto God, defer not to pay it; for [he hath] no pleasure in fools: pay that which thou hast vowed.
5. *Better [is it] that thou shouldest not vow, than that thou shouldest vow and not pay*.
6. [NLT] Don't let your mouth make you sin. And ***don't defend yourself by telling the Temple messenger (priest) that the promise you made was a mistake***. That would make God angry, and he might wipe out everything you have achieved.
7. [NLT] Talk is cheap, like daydreams and other useless activities. Fear God instead.

In Ecclesiastes 5:6, we see the writer explaining that once a vow has been made, the defense of "I made a mistake" would be rejected by the court (the priest). The court would treat such a claim as a valid neder (binding vow) as opposed to a mistaken vow neder b'ta'ut (a vow made in error). This is the same concept Jesus emphasized in Matthew 5:37.

In Matthew 23:16–22, Jesus further addressed the misguided teachings of the Pharisees and scribes concerning oaths. They had developed a system that distinguished between binding and non-binding oaths based on what one swore by. According to their tradition, swearing by the temple, the altar, or by heaven itself was considered non-binding, while swearing by the gold of the temple or the gift on the altar made the oath binding. Jesus rebuked this hypocrisy and faulty reasoning. He emphasized that it is not the gold or the gift that holds intrinsic value, but rather the sacredness of the temple and the altar that sanctifies them. Therefore, the temple is greater than the gold, and the altar is greater than the gift. Jesus' point is clear: all oaths are serious, and one's word must be kept regardless of the specifics of the vow. Jesus said the Pharisees and Scribes would travel by land and sea to convert one person to Judaism, but by teaching these loopholes, they were making the convert (proselyte) "twice as much a child of hell as they were" (Matthew 23:15.

As Psalm 15:4 reminds us, a righteous person "keeps an oath even when it hurts, and does not change their mind." Integrity requires that we honor our commitments, even when doing so comes at personal cost.

"Till Death do we Part" and Breaking Vows

When the couple makes the vow to be married, stating "till death do us part" has become customary. The phrase "till death do us part" was added to the wedding vow by Bishop Thomas Cranmer in the mid-1500s as part of the Reformation of the Church of England. And yet Cranmer was complicit in enabling King Henry VIII's divorce, convening a special ecclesiastical court at Dunstable Priory, declaring Henry's marriage of 23 years to Catherine null and void, and validating Henry's marriage to Anne Boleyn, which had taken place in secret before the divorce was valid. Many believe this decision eventually led to Cranmer being burned at the stake by Mary, the daughter of King Henry, once she became queen. As a cleric, Thomas Cranmer broke the Catholic rules of clerical celibacy. Around 1532, while serving as a diplomat in Germany, he secretly married Margarete Osiander. At that time, Catholic canon law still forbade priests from marrying, so his marriage violated his vow of celibacy.

Unfortunately, too much emphasis has been placed on this singular phrase, while the other commitments within the vow are often overlooked.

The covenant of marriage is based on each statement of the agreement made, such as to honor, to have, to hold, and so on. Breaking any one of these commitments breaks the covenant. The scriptures use the word "tenor" to describe this.

Exodus 34:27 (KJV)
And the Lord said unto Moses, Write thou these words: for after ***the tenor*** of these words I have made a covenant with thee and with Israel.

The word "tenor" refers to the terms of the covenant. A marriage has terms; it is not a lifelong commitment without an agreement.

Does breaking the "tenor" mean a divorce is now required? No, repentance and forgiveness are required. Refusing to repent means that one or both parties of the covenant are backsliding. The word "backsliding" means apostasy, which refers to the act of refusing to continue to follow or obey the agreement. While there is still room for repentance, true repentance means to change one's mind, turn from sin, feel regret or contrition, and dedicate oneself to amend. If a person continues to break or breach the agreement, the covenant is ultimately ended, kārat. It is impossible for two to walk together if they do not agree.

God ended His agreement with Israel. He breached His promise because Israel refused to keep their part, which was to believe in Him. Once Israel backslid, God breached the promise.

Numbers 14:34 (KJV)
After the number of the days in which ye searched the land, [even] forty days, each day for a year, shall ye bear your iniquities, [even] forty years, and ***ye shall know my breach of promise***.

In Jeremiah 3:8, the system of divorce is outlined for us. By committing an act that breached the covenant—adultery in this case—Israel first backslid. Their refusal to change (repentance with godly sorrow) led to them being put away and given a bill of divorcement.

Jeremiah 3:8 (KJV)
And I saw, when for all the causes whereby backsliding Israel
committed adultery I had put her away, and given her a bill of
divorce; yet her treacherous sister Judah feared not, but went and
played the harlot also.

These four parts constitute the system of divorce: An act that breaks
the agreement leads to backsliding, which will eventually lead to separation
(putting away) and ultimately divorce. Of course, this is only the case if
there is no repentance, forgiveness, or restoration.

SO, HOW DO WE HANDLE DIVORCE?

Well, the Scriptures provide two opposing stories as examples. We have Hosea, the prophet, whose wife was unfaithful to him, and the Lord required him to go after her, establishing a new covenant. She represented Israel, being a wife to God. On the other hand, we have Ezra, where God did not require forgiveness; they were required to put away their wives. Though many claim that God required them to put away their wives because they were foreigners or pagan, the law required these women to follow the ways of God, and they didn't—unlike Ruth or Rahab, who made the God of Israel their God. Hosea's wife also did not follow the ways of God, so that argument is not adequate to use scripture alone as a guide.

In 1 Corinthians 7, the apostle Paul corrected the church at Corinth after they had embraced the idea that celibacy led to a higher level of spirituality — even within marriage. This is why Paul instructed husbands and wives not to deprive (or defraud) each other. Some believers had already divorced, and Paul told them to reconcile, since their divorces were not the result of unresolved sin or conflict. Even after a divorce decree had been issued, Paul encouraged reconciliation and remarriage, which was considered normal within the Jewish community. In halakhah (Jewish law), if a man divorces his wife, he is permitted — and even encouraged — to remarry her if both desire reconciliation. The Talmud refers to this as machazir gerushato, which literally means "returning his divorcee."

How do we know which example we should follow? We are to be led by the Spirit of God. Pray until there is certainty that it is the Lord. Leaving a spouse because of an unrighteous motive is not the Lord. Remaining in a relationship through physical, emotional, or psychological abuse and torment is not the Lord's will either. The idea of "for better or worse" does not include being subjected to physical or emotional abuse.

Doesn't God Hate Divorce?

Well, the Scripture actually says God hates the "putting away" (šālah), which means sending away. The Hebrew word for divorce, kᵊrîṯûṯ or kāraṯ, is not used in that passage.

It's important to understand the context behind the statement, "God hates divorce." The prophet Malachi was sent by God to correct the priests, who were treating their wives "treacherously." They were mishandling their wives, and God sent the prophet to tell them to be better husbands. God told them to stop being unfaithful husbands. God had refused to hear the prayers of these priests because of how they mistreated their wives. These priests were on the verge of being labeled mored (rebellious husbands).

Malachi 2:14-16 (NLT)

14. *You cry out, "Why doesn't the LORD accept my worship?" I'll tell you why!* Because the LORD witnessed the vows you and your wife made when you were young. But *you have been unfaithful to her*, though *she remained your faithful partner*, the wife of your marriage vows.

15. Didn't the LORD make you one with your wife? In body and spirit you are his. *And what does he want? Godly children from your union*. So guard your heart; remain loyal to the wife of your youth.

16. "For I hate divorce!" says the LORD, the God of Israel. "To divorce your wife is to overwhelm her with cruelty," says the LORD of Heaven's Armies. "So guard your heart; ***do not be unfaithful to your wife.***"

The Christian response to the above passage would be that these priests must have been cheating on their wives. However, "unfaithful" does not necessarily mean adultery; if it did, these priests would have been brought to court, and these women would have been granted a divorce according to the law of Moses. Unfaithfulness to the vow is what constitutes unfaithfulness in marriage. God highlights the fact that these men were not having children with their wives. He desired "Godly offspring" (Malachi 2:15). God does not hear the prayers of husbands who mistreat their wives. Malachi explained this to the priests in verse 14, as they had been crying out to God, but God would not answer them. Peter explains the same principle in the New Testament.

1 Peter 3:7 (KJV)
Likewise, ye ***husbands***, dwell with [them] according to knowledge, ***giving honour unto the wife***, as unto the weaker vessel, and as being heirs together of the grace of life; ***that your prayers be not hindered***.

God does not want husbands to mistreat or abuse their wives, nor does He want wives to mistreat their husbands. For marriage to thrive, it must be built on honor.

By treating your spouse with honor, an unusual and undeserved respect, you will avoid mistreating one another. How you speak to and respond to someone you hold in high esteem changes your tone, word choice, actions, and behavior. You do not degrade, dismiss, disrespect, purposely embarrass, or insult someone you honor.

1 Peter 3:5-7 (NLT)

5. This is how the holy women of old made themselves beautiful. They trusted God and accepted the authority of their husbands.

6. For instance, Sarah obeyed her husband, Abraham, and called him her master. You are her daughters when you do what is right without fear of what your husbands might do.

7. In the same way, you husbands must give honor to your wives. Treat your wife with understanding as you live together. She may be weaker than you are, but she is your equal partner in God's gift of new life. Treat her as you should so your prayers will not be hindered.

We cannot preach legalism, take a strict anti-divorce stance, and call it God's will. Unfortunately, divorce is sometimes a necessary evil because some men and women have hard hearts. They refuse to repent and change. Some never see themselves as being the problem or accept accountability. Some are extremely selfish, while others are so broken that the marriage has become destructive and toxic. Many people avoid the healing needed to create strong, healthy marriages. Some marry for ulterior motives that the other person isn't aware of until later. Other couples face such challenging circumstances that the relationship has no chance of survival.

The effects of sin have made marriage challenging. But God never intended marriage to be just between a man and a woman; He was always meant to be a part of the equation. God did not meet with Adam alone in the garden; He met with Adam and Eve. This was always the formula for marriage.

Marriage requires repentance, forgiveness, restoration, respect, honor, honesty, trust, compassion, compromise, discipline, consistency, constancy, fidelity, gentleness, and more. Sadly, not everyone has the maturity for marriage or seeks God's help to make it work. When one party refuses to honor their commitment, the relationship may be over. Once the tenor (terms of agreement) has been broken, then the covenant has ended. The covenant would need to be reestablished, or the two parties would go their separate ways. This is what Jesus referred to as the hardness of men's hearts — the refusal to change or take accountability.

In Israel, after the priests tried reconciling the marriage, if a spouse was deemed to be rebellious, the couple would be compelled to divorce. So, as Paul stated, if you are bound (married) to a wife, do not seek a divorce. But if you are released or divorced, do not seek to remarry. However, if you do remarry, you have not sinned.

1 Corinthians 7:27-28 (NET)

27. The one bound to a wife should not seek divorce. The one released from a wife should not seek marriage.

28. But if you marry, you have not sinned...

GOD THOUGHT SO

In Judaism, divorce is commonly viewed as a necessary evil. Rabbis often reference several Scriptures—not to justify divorce, but to acknowledge the very real challenges of marriage. While many of these verses highlight the woman's disposition, the principles can certainly apply to men with similar temperaments.

Proverbs 21:9 (KJV)
It is better to dwell in a corner of the housetop, than with a
brawling woman in a wide house.

Proverbs 21:19 (KJV)
It is better to dwell in the wilderness, than with a contentious and
an angry woman.

Proverbs 27:15 (KJV)
A continual dropping in a very rainy day and a contentious woman
are alike.

Proverbs 30:21–23 (KJV)
21. For three things the earth is disquieted, and for four which it
cannot bear:
22. For a servant when he reigneth; and a fool when he is filled
with meat;
23. For an odious [bitter, hateful, unloved] woman when she is
married; and an handmaid that is heir to her mistress.

Even the New Testament echoes this theme of emotional balance and compassion in marriage. In Colossians 3:19, husbands are admonished to guard their hearts against bitterness:

Colossians 3:19 (KJV)
Husbands, love your wives, and be not bitter against them.

These verses remind us that marriage requires grace, patience, and mutual responsibility. While Scripture acknowledges the difficulty that can arise in relationships, it also offers wisdom for navigating those tensions with godly character and love.

So, what does divorce look like in Jewish culture? A Jewish divorce is performed by a Beit Din (a rabbinical court), typically consisting of three rabbinic judges (or more, depending on the situation). These judges, who are well-versed in Jewish law (halacha), ensure that the proper procedures are followed for the divorce to be valid. A scribe is present to write the bill of divorcement (the get) on behalf of the husband. Two witnesses must also be present, and they cannot be family members. The language used in a Jewish bill of divorcement or get is very interesting. Below are some key lines from a get:

"I willingly consent to... release, discharge, and divorce you..." "This shall be for you from me a bill of dismissal, a letter of release, and a document of absolution, in accordance with the law of Moses and Israel." Some documents add Miriam's name after Moses.

The divorce service performed by the rabbis is meant to bring closure. I find the last statement especially interesting: "A document of absolution." Jewish divorces address the "sin factor" in their bill of divorce.

The Merriam-Webster Dictionary defines "absolution" as "the act of forgiving someone for having done something wrong or sinful: the act of absolving someone or the state of being absolved." Specifically, it refers to "a remission of sins pronounced by a priest (as in the sacrament of reconciliation)."

In preparation for a Jewish divorce, the priests may fast. During the procedure, prayers are recited, songs are sung, and scriptures are read. There is a prayer of forgiveness that the couple says together or separately to one another. Although there are several prayers and steps apart from the Judaic divorce service, I will focus on the prayer of forgiveness.

"A Ritual for Ending a Marriage" by Rabbi Rachel Barenblat - The Prayer for Forgiveness.

The divorcing couple speaks these words, either in turn or simultaneously:

"Eternal Friend, witness that I forgive [Name] for any injuries sustained over the course of our relationship, whether by accident or willfully, carelessly, or purposely with words, deeds, thoughts, or attitudes now or in previous incarnations. May s/he not experience harm because of me. May the words of my mouth and the meditations of my heart be acceptable to You, Who protects and frees me."

This prayer of forgiveness, done in the presence of a priest, brings closure to the marriage. Forgiveness and closure are key pieces that many never experience following a divorce.

The divorce rate among Jews is lower than that of Americans, which is around 50%. The Religious Demographics of Divorce in the United States (January 31, 2024) by Adam Sacks (sacksandsackslaw.com) lists the divorce rate at 51% for Protestant Christians, whereas Orthodox Jews have a 9% rate. There is clearly something different about how marriage is viewed and experienced in the Jewish community, particularly those who follow the Torah, compared to Christian culture "following the Bible." I do not see the same level of seriousness placed on marriage in the Christian community as I do in the Jewish community. The willingness to involve the community and the roles that rabbis play in their homes and marriages provide lasting support.

I do not propose that we follow the Jewish system. To follow that system, we must adopt the entire law of Moses, and we are not under the law. However, I believe that just as the system was designed to be an example and shadow (Hebrews 5:8), there are key components that we may need to adopt in Christian culture.

It is my belief that because Christian marriage is done before a minister, but we allow divorce to be handled only through secular courts, closure and healing take much longer. Moses, as instructed by God, required God's blessing in both marriage and divorce. Am I crazy for proposing that divorce should be done in the presence of God? Divorce was required to be done in the presence of priests, so apparently, God thought so.

INDEX